FOCUS GROUPS

FOCUS GROUPS

A Practical Guide for Applied Research

RICHARD A. KRUEGER

Foreword by Michael Quinn Patton

SAGE PUBLICATIONS
The Publishers of Professional Social Science
Newbury Park   Beverly Hills   London   New Delhi

For information address:

SAGE Publications, Inc.
2111 West Hillcrest Drive
Newbury Park, California 91320

SAGE Publications Inc.   SAGE Publications Ltd.
275 South Beverly Drive   28 Banner Street
Beverly Hills   London EC1Y 8QE
California 90212   England

SAGE PUBLICATIONS India Pvt. Ltd.
M-32 Market
Greater Kailash I
New Delhi 110 048 India

Printed in the United States of America

Library of Congress Cataloging-in-Publication Data

Krueger, Richard A.
  Focus groups: a practical guide for applied research / by
Richard A. Krueger.
     p.   cm.
  Bibliography: p.
  Includes index.
  ISBN 0-8039-3186-7   ISBN 0-8039-3187-5 (pbk.)
  1. Evaluation research (Social action programs) I. Title.
H62.K754 1988   87-33413
361.6′1′068—dc19   CIP

FIRST PRINTING 1988

Contents

Foreword

This book represents more than a comprehensive and detailed presentation of a specific methodological approach. This careful and thorough analysis of focus group interviewing techniques also adds a new dimension of methodological eclecticism and diversity to professional evaluation practice.

Evaluation has emerged as a distinct field of professional practice. One characteristic of this new field is its methodological diversity. That diversity is an outgrowth of evaluators' commitment to providing useful information for program improvement and decision making.

Evaluators must be able to use a variety of methods and techniques to get timely information to decision makers about program processes and outcomes. Focus group interviewing is an important part of a responsive evaluator's repertoire because it has particular advantages in providing in-depth information from the perspective of program participants about their needs, interests, and concerns. It is a relatively cost-effective technique because it brings together a number of people at one point in time to provide data on highly focused topics. While it is an approach that can be used alone, focus group interviews are often employed with other methods both quantitative and qualitative.

Richard Krueger was one of the first evaluators to begin seriously studying the relevance of market research experiences with focus group interviews for application to program evaluation problems. He has made extensive use of focus groups in his own evaluation work. One of the strengths of this book is the wealth of examples Dick uses to illustrate the various facets of focus group interviewing and data analysis.

He has also built on the experiences of private sector market researchers who regularly apply these techniques. The Twin Cities of Minneapolis and St. Paul are a market research haven with a number of firms making heavy use of focus group techniques. Dick has studied that work in developing this approach for applied social science and evaluation purposes.

Like any technique, focus groups exemplify both strengths and weaknesses. The surface simplicity of the approach may make it easily subject to abuse. In this book, Dick shows that surface simplicity is deceiving. Used casually and without careful preparation, the resulting data may not be worth using. Used carefully and appropriately, the results of focus group interviews can be quite powerful and useful. This book makes clear what the difference is. In so doing, this book is an important contribution to the methodological development of program evaluation.

> —*Michael Quinn Patton*
> President
> American Evaluation Association

Preface

I wrote this book after agonizing over the lack of recent literature available to the evaluation researcher on focus group interviewing. Most of what is known about focus group interviewing has been in the hands of a guild of practitioners with the technique passed down from master to apprentice. Unfortunately, this inefficient process of information transfer results in limited availability for those researchers who are unable to watch the masters.

Much of what is known about focus groups comes primarily from market research, where the procedure has flourished in the past several decades. I have made an attempt to draw from these areas and also from the fields of psychology, sociology, and other social sciences. The book pays particular attention to the use of focus group interviewing within the nonprofit sector. Increasingly, all organizations (profit and nonprofit alike) are becoming concerned about listening to the client, customer, or user of products, programs, or services. Within the nonprofit sector, however, several features of focus groups receive differing emphasis. For example, the use of assistant moderators, the added value of the listening process to the sponsoring organization, and the strategies of recruitment represent modifications typically used in the nonprofit sector. Moreover, nonprofit organizations are beginning to discover the values of marketing their opportunities and this book should prove helpful in that regard.

More than anything else, this book presents an alternative means of obtaining information from people. Decision makers regularly encounter this problem as they seek to plan, administer, or allocate resources. It has been my experience that the first reaction of decision makers is to request a survey. In part, this reaction is prompted by two factors: the survey's scientific aura and the decision maker's lack of knowledge about alternative means of gathering information. Focus groups offer an alternative that capitalizes on the strengths of the decision makers: knowledge of the program and an ability to talk to clientele.

The book was developed after an extensive literature search; observation of both masters and novices as they engage in focus groups; and experiences in classes, workshops, and seminars designed to help nonresearchers develop the requisite skills for moderating focus groups. The tenor of the suggestions will emphasize the practical considerations of moderating more than the theoretical underpinnings of focus group interviews. It is hoped that the book will also serve as a review to those researchers who are already grounded in the basics of moderating.

The book is organized around three themes. Part I (Chapters 1 and 2) presents a general overview of focus groups that highlights distinctions between this methodological procedure and other seemingly similar group or individual research procedures. Within Part I, the reader will find a discussion of the development of focus group procedures, why focus groups work, characteristics of focus groups, uses of focus groups, validity of focus group interviewing, and advantages and limitations of this research procedure. This first part of the book is intended to provide the readers—both researchers and users—with the concepts that undergird focus group interviewing.

Part II (Chapters 3 through 8) suggests strategies for actually conducting focus group interviews. This section of the book emphasizes the elements involved in doing focus groups and will likely be of greater interest to researchers as they prepare for the experience. Chapter 3 highlights the conceptualization and planning necessary for successful focus groups. Effective focus groups depend upon quality questions (Chapter 4), moderating skills (Chapter 5), and involvement of the right participants (Chapter 6). Analysis procedures are presented in Chapter 7, followed by reporting focus group results in Chapter 8.

Part III brings to light several issues that are often of concern to both researchers and users, particularly those within the nonprofit sector. Chapter 9 discusses the involvement of nonresearchers in the focus group interview process, Chapter 10 suggests several variations of focus groups that have proven to be effective, and Chapter 11 provides suggestions for contracting for focus group assistance.

I owe much to colleagues and friends who have assisted me with this effort. While the title page bears the name of a single author, the contents would not have been possible without the contributions of others. Michael Q. Patton, scholar, teacher, and friend, has provided encouragement, sound advice, and enthusiasm for the book. It has been my good fortune to conduct a number of focus group workshops with Marsha R. Mueller. Her astute perceptions and helpful suggestions contributed much to this work. Mary Anne Casey was a valuable critic who helped me straighten out the logic and then reviewed early drafts to ensure that the details were correct. Sandra Becker helped in arranging the ideas to achieve a readable style. Sandra's skills in written communication provided substantial improvements in the manuscript. Ed Nelson, an expert in obtaining information, contributed thoughtful and generous advice that strengthened the manuscript. Randy Cantrell provided methodological expertise and carefully reviewed the final draft.

Colleagues within the division of agricultural education at the University of Minnesota assisted in the effort. Professor Roland Peterson enthusiastically provided suggestions after using focus group procedures in new situations. Edgar Persons, head of the division of agricultural education, provided encouragement throughout the writing stages. Graduate students Theresa Ahles, Jerry Migler, Suleiman Ngware, and Peter Scheffert contributed ideas and advice that were of substantial benefit.

I am indebted to colleagues with the Cooperative Extension Service who were willing to try out the ideas and suggest refinements to the procedures described in this book. Through field application, I have had the opportunity to learn from many individuals, including Shirley Barber, Greg Hutchins, Brent Larson, Nancy Lenhart, Sheryl Nefstead, Joan Sprain, Eric Vogel, and Charlie Walkinshaw from Minnesota; Pamela Kutara, Rhonda Lincoln, Charlotte Nakamura, and Rhoda Yoshino from Hawaii; Tom Archer and Jeff Layman from Ohio; Jim Long from Washington; and Sue Sadowske from Wisconsin. Pat Borich, dean and director of the Minnesota Cooperative Extension Service, has provided steady and consistent encouragement and support for program evaluation in the public sector.

Jackie Admire and Larry Bell provided insights in using focus groups within the medical community; Ardis Cook Hutchins and Gail Olney within the area of architecture and interior design; Elizabeth Smith, Don Stoike, Wayne Rydberg, and Bill Busching within the nonprofit fraternal benefit organization; Ed Nelson within natural resources; and Sue Krueger within the public school environment.

My wife Sue believed from the start that the book would get finished and helped arrange a home life that would allow for uninterrupted writing. In addition, she provided constant encouragement, helpful advice, and necessary support to complete the manuscript. Sara and Peter were principal sources of information on teen focus groups and helped their dad understand how teens think.

—Richard A. Krueger

Part I

Groups and Focus Groups

FIRST EXPOSURE TO A FOCUS GROUP

Betty was relaxing at home after a hectic day at the office. She just finished reading Section A of today's newspaper and is reaching for Section B when the telephone rings. She answers, expecting a call from her brother George.

"Hello."

"Good evening," the voice on the phone responds. "I'm conducting a survey of people in the community, and I would like to ask you a few questions. It will only take a couple minutes. Is it OK to begin?"

"Sure, go ahead."

"Do you have any houseplants in your home?" the caller asks.

"Yes," Betty answers.

"How many do you have? Would you say that you have less than five plants, five to ten plants, or more than ten plants?" the voice inquires.

"More than ten."

"In the past year, have you used any fertilizer or plant growth chemicals on your plants?"

"Yes, I have," she responds.

"Our company, which is Research Incorporated, is conducting a study of houseplant fertilizer. We would like to invite you to a special meeting to discuss fertilizer products. There will be no selling involved, and if you decide to attend we will provide you with a year's supply of plant fertilizer. The meeting will be held on January 12 from 7:00 to 8:30 p.m. It will be at the Hanover Motel in Minneapolis. Would you be able to join us?"

"Sure, count me in," Betty replies.

"Great. Now let me get your name and address . . ."

It all happened rather quickly, and, after the call is over, Betty began to wonder what it was all about. "A year's supply of fertilizer is great, but what's the catch? They said no selling was involved, but why would they want to hold a meeting to discuss fertilizer on houseplants? Oh well, I guess I'll just have to wait and find out."

Does this phone call sound familiar? The call was a telephone screening questionnaire for a focus group. Betty passed through the screens for selection and accepted the invitation to talk about houseplant fertilizer. If she didn't have houseplants or use fertilizer, she would have received a polite, "Thank you, we have no further questions," and the call would have ended.

Later, after the meeting, Betty's brother George asked her about the experience. She reflected: "The meeting was interesting, in fact enjoyable. There were about ten people there, including a person who asked questions. The people all had houseplants and talked about different types of fertilizer. The discussion leader asked questions about fertilizer and seemed particularly interested in the reasons why we selected various brands, and what we liked about different types of fertilizer. At the end of the session, the leader told us the information would be used by the Northern Fertilizer Company to improve their product. Before I left, I was offered either two gallons of liquid houseplant fertilizer or a five pound bag of dry fertilizer."

Betty experienced a focus group interview. It is one of the most popular tools in market research today. A growing number of people have participated in focus groups. Interestingly, however, many participants in Betty's group didn't know that the group discussion was a focus group interview or that the telephone survey was a screen for focus group participation. Rarely is the term *focus group* used at the group discussion, because the term might inhibit the spontaneous comments of participants. Also the term *focus group* is rarely used when invitations are made to potential participants. Instead participants are invited to "discuss" or "share ideas with others," thereby conveying the informal nature of the discussion.

Focus groups are increasingly being used by researchers to discover preferences for new or existing products. The focus group discussion is particularly effective in providing information about *why* people think or feel the way they do.

THE QUEST FOR INFORMATION

Focus groups have been a mainstay in private sector marketing research. More recently, public sector organizations are beginning to discover the potential of this procedure. Educational and nonprofit organizations have traditionally used face-to-face interviews and questionnaires to get information. Unfortunately, these popular techniques are sometimes inadequate in meeting information needs of decision makers. The focus group is unique from these other procedures; it allows for group interaction and greater insight into why certain opinions are held. Focus groups can improve the planning and design of new programs, provide means of evaluating existing programs, and produce insights for developing marketing strategies. This book is intended to provide assistance in using focus groups to obtain information that will be helpful to decision makers.

1

Groups

Groups are a common experience. It would be difficult to find a human being who has not been in a group; indeed, most of us are repeatedly confronted with a plethora of groups. We find ourselves invited, herded, or seduced into groups for planning, decision making, advising, brainstorming, self-help, and a host of other purposes.

It's not surprising that we think twice at the prospect of getting together in a group. Groups can be fun, exciting, or invigorating, but they can also be agonizing, time-consuming experiences that are both unproductive and unnecessary. In some organizational environments, the group (task force, committee, and so on) is created because individuals are confused as to a future course of action. More often than not, the pooled confusion does not result in enlightenment, but only more confusion. As a result, the group becomes our scapegoat—we blame the group for the fallibilities of the individuals in the group. The group is neither good nor bad, but merely a reflection of our human capabilities. The group magnifies our individual wisdom or short-comings. Our shortcomings are often the result of confusion about the purpose and process of the group.

Sometimes the purpose of the group is clearly understood, such as in a nominating committee where the end result is a slate of officer candidates. Other times, the purpose of the group is vaguely understood, perceived differently by participants, or changed over time. We tend to engage in group experiences without careful thought or clarity of purpose. At times, the function of the group may be to suggest ideas, to clarify potential options, to recommend a course of action, or to make a decision—each function considerably different from the others. Re-searchers regularly find themselves working with groups for purposes of planning or evaluating. Difficulties emerge when there is ambiguity on these endeavors. At different times, a group might function as a task force, as a working group to develop instruments or in interpreting results. Lack of clarity in defining the group purpose can result in confusion, misunderstandings, wasted time, and—most likely—the wrong conclusions.

The second type of confusion relates to the group process. Group leaders may not have the necessary skills to guide the group process. Effective leadership is essential if the group is to accomplish its purpose. The group leader must not only be in tune with the purpose of the group but also have the necessary skills to guide the group process effectively. Furthermore, the skills necessary for one type of group experience do not necessarily transfer into other group settings.

THE FOCUS GROUP:
A SPECIAL TYPE OF GROUP

The focus group is a special type of group in terms of purpose, size, composition, and procedures. A focus group is typically composed of seven to ten participants who are unfamiliar with each other. These participants are selected because they have certain characteristics in common that relate to the topic of the focus group.

The researcher creates a permissive environment in the focus group that nurtures different perceptions and points of view, without pressuring participants to vote, plan, or reach consensus. The group discussion is conducted several times with similar types of participants to identify trends and patterns in perceptions. Careful and systematic analysis of the discussions provide clues and insights as to how a product, service, or opportunity is perceived.

In summary, a focus group can be defined as a carefully planned discussion designed to obtain perceptions on a defined area of interest in a permissive, nonthreatening environment. It is conducted with approximately seven to ten people by a skilled interviewer. The discussion is relaxed, comfortable, and often enjoyable for participants as they share their ideas and perceptions. Group members influence each other by responding to ideas and comments in the discussion.

THE STORY BEHIND
FOCUS GROUP INTERVIEWS

Focus group interviews were born out of necessity. In the late 1930s, social scientists began investigating the values of nondirective individual interviewing as an improved source of information. They had doubts about the accuracy of traditional information gathering methods, specifically the excessive influence of the interviewer and the limitations of predetermined, closed-ended questions. The traditional individual interview, which used a predetermined questionnaire with closed-ended response choices, had a major disadvantage: The respondent was limited by the choices offered and, therefore, the findings could be unintentionally influenced by the interviewer by oversight or omission. By contrast, nondirective procedures begin with limited assumptions and place considerable emphasis on getting in tune with the reality of the interviewee. Moreover, the nondirective interviews used open-ended questions and allowed individuals to respond without setting boundaries or providing clues for potential response categories. The open-ended approaches allow the subject ample opportunity to comment, to explain, and to share experiences and attitudes as opposed to the structured and directive interview that is dominated by the interviewer. Stuart A. Rice was one of the first social scientists to express concern. In 1931, he wrote:

> A defect of the interview for the purposes of fact-finding in scientific research, then, is that the questioner takes the lead. That is, the subject plays a more or less passive role. Information or points of view of the highest value may not be disclosed because the direction given the interview by the questioner leads away from them. In short, data obtained from an interview are as likely to embody the preconceived ideas of the interviewer as the attitude of the subject interviewed. (Rice, 1931, p. 561)

As a result social scientists began considering strategies whereby the researcher would take on a less directive and dominating role and the respondent would be able to comment on the areas deemed by that respondent to be most important. In effect, the emphasis of nondirective interviewing was to shift attention from the interviewer to the respondent.

Nondirective interviewing had particular appeal to social scientists and psychologists in the late 1930s and 1940s. Roethlisberger and Dickson (1938) cited it in studies of employee motivation and Carl Rogers (1942) in psychotherapy. During World War II, increased attention was placed on focused interviewing in groups, primarily as a means of increasing military morale. Many of the procedures that have come to be accepted as common practice in focus group interviews were set forth in the classic work by Robert K. Merton, Marjorie Fiske, and Patricia L. Kendall, *The Focused Interview* (1956).

In the past thirty years, most applications of focus group interviewing have been in market research. Those who develop or manufacture new products know the importance of advertising their products, and are also well aware of the financial risks of introducing new products. Gone are the days when emphasis was placed on super salespeople who could sell anything. The sensible strategy is to stay in touch with people. Focus group interviews have considerable value because they enable the producers, manufacturers, and sellers to understand the thinking of the consumers.

Most recently, focus group interviews have been regarded by many as a crucial step in shaping the marketing strategy for products. Coe and MacLachlan (1980) found that focus groups were the most popular technique for evaluating television commercials among the 37 largest users of television advertising. Some products have undergone major revisions in manufacturing, packaging, or advertising due to findings in focus groups. Advertising campaigns often highlight what the consumer considers to be the positive attributes of the product. For example, soft drink companies discovered via focus groups that consumers drink beverages not because of thirst, but because of the sociability features associated with the product. It is no wonder then that slogans promoting these beverages highlight how "things go better" or increased personal popularity on the beach (Bellenger, Bernhardt, & Goldstrucker, 1976).

Recently, focus groups have been found to be useful beyond the area of advertising. Robert Vichas (1983) offers two examples. A movie studio that has received numerous awards and quintupled profits in five years regularly uses focus groups to test audience reactions to possible endings for new films. Also, a firm that had considered manufacturing automobile air-conditioning filters had scrubbed the idea after conducting focus groups. Customers did not see the need for the filter, would not pay the price, and had fears about how it would affect the car air conditioner. The small investment in focus groups saved the company from making a very costly and unprofitable investment in a new product.

Focus group interviews are widely accepted within marketing research because they produce believable results at a reasonable cost. This technique is growing in popularity among other information seekers, such as social scientists, evaluators, planners, and educators. It is a particularly appropriate procedure to use when the goal is to explain how people regard an experience, idea, or event.

Social scientists are finally rediscovering the focus group. Merton's pioneering work has lain dormant in the social sciences for decades. The evolution of focus groups, and, for that matter, of qualitative research methods in general, has been delayed for a variety of reasons—a preoccupation with quantitative procedures, assumptions about the nature of reality, and a societal tendency to believe in numbers. For several decades, the pendulum of evaluation research has swung to the quantitative side with primary attention to experimental designs, control groups, and randomization. This sojourn with numbers has been beneficial in that we have gained in our experimental sophistication, but it also nurtured a desire for more understanding of the human experience. Too often the quantitative approaches were based on assumptions about people, about things, or about reality in general that were not warranted.

The process of evaluating social programs is maturing, in part because of an environment that expects relevance, practicality, and utility. Increasingly, human service programs are requested to be more accountable for the resources they consume. Those directing educational, medical, and social programs are being asked to document what they are doing and the impact of their efforts on people. Failure to take accountability seriously can have deleterious consequences on future funding. As a result, public and private providers of services are increasingly interested in knowing more about how their clients (customers) view their programs. Strategic planning, needs assessment, and program evaluation are critical activities for human service professionals who want to improve programs and services. Focus groups can provide them information about perceptions, feelings, and attitudes of program clients. The procedure allows professionals to see reality from the client's point of view.

For example, the University of Minnesota College of Agriculture was concerned about its declining enrollment of rural youth. High school graduates from small rural Minnesota schools were enrolling in agricultural colleges in neighboring states. A series of focus groups with potential students revealed that the young people had some negative notions about the university, and, in fact, the university was unwittingly adding to their erroneous perceptions. Students from small rural high schools saw the University of Minnesota as too big and too impersonal. They felt that they would get lost in the thousands of students at the university and, therefore, they preferred smaller schools. With this insight, the faculty in the division of agricultural education took another look at the promotional materials being distributed to prospective students. The descriptive brochures had numerous pictures of the university—pictures of the campus mall with thousands of students and pictures showing the grandeur of the university. The brochures told of the millions of books in the library, the thousands of students in the university, and the scores and scores of departments and majors. Clearly, the existing promotional materials reinforced the fears of potential students. As a result of focus group research, faculty members designed a special brochure that emphasized the "more compact" St. Paul campus, "friendly teachers who take an interest in you," and the benefits of attending college with other students from rural communities (Casey et al., 1987).

It is dangerous for a university, or for any public service agency, to take the customer for granted. Periodically, effort is needed to get in touch with the customer and see the agency, program, service, or institution from the perspective of the client. Patricia Labaw, in her text on survey design, argues that the day of "seat-of-the-pants decision making" has ended. She writes:

> Whether we choose to recognize it or not, our society is basically marketing oriented. None of our institutions exists indefinitely on public sufferance; each must perform. Each must respond to need. As a consequence every policymaker must know what the need is and try to learn the best way of providing the service or product to meet the need. The days of seat-of-the-pants decision making are passing, if they have not indeed already passed. (Labaw, 1985, p. 17)

A similar view is expressed by Daniel Katz et al. in *Bureaucratic Encounters* (1975, p. 2); they argue:

> In private enterprise under competitive conditions, there is some direct feedback from the appropriate public when people exercise their discretionary power as consumers to purchase from one or another competing source. In private monopolies and public agencies, there is no such direct check on products or services. In such cases the need for systematic feedback from the people being served is all the more necessary.

Administrators of nonprofit institutions are taking their cues from the private sector and discovering that marketing the product is essential. While some institutions are able to survive on their historic reputation, other nonprofit organizations are concerned about maintaining or increasing their audience and meeting client needs in the most efficient manner possible. The trend is not unique to nonprofits. Peters and Waterman's examination of excellence in American business attributes a portion of the private sectors' success to staying in tune with the customer.

WHY DO FOCUS GROUPS WORK?

The focus group interview works because it taps into human tendencies. Attitudes and perceptions relating to products, services, or programs are developed in part by interaction with other people. We are a product of our environment and are influenced by people around us. A deficiency of mail and telephone surveys and even face-to-face interviews is that those methods assume that individuals really do know how they feel. A further assumption is that individuals form opinions in isolation. Both of these assumptions have presented problems for researchers. People may need to listen to opinions of others before they form their own personal viewpoints. While some opinions may be developed quickly and held with absolute certainty, other opinions are malleable and dynamic. Evidence from focus group interviews suggests that people do influence each other with their comments, and, in the course of a discussion, the opinions of an individual might shift. The focus group analyst can thereby discover more about how that shift occurred and the nature of the influencing factors.

Often, the questions asked in a focused interview are deceptively simple. They are the kinds of questions an individual could answer in a couple of minutes. When questions are asked in a group environment and nourished by skillful probing, the results are candid portraits of customer perceptions. The permissive group environment gives individuals license to divulge emotions that often do not emerge in other forms of questioning. Indeed, one of the hazards in getting information from people is that they often want to tell us how they wish to be seen as opposed to how they are.

The intent of the focus group is to promote self-disclosure among participants. For some individuals, self-disclosure comes easily—it is natural and comfortable. But for others, it is difficult or uncomfortable and requires trust, effort, and courage. Children have a natural tendency to disclose things about themselves but through socialization they learn the values of dissembling. Over time, the natural and spontaneous disclosures of children are modified by social pressure. Sidney Jourard expands on this tendency:

> As children we are, and we act, our real selves. We say what we think, we scream for what we want, we tell what we did. These spontaneous disclosures meet variable consequences—some disclosures are ignored, some rewarded, and some punished. Doubtless in accordance with the laws of reinforcement, we learn early to withhold certain disclosures

because of the painful consequences to which they lead. We are punished in our society, not only for what we actually do, but also for what we think, feel, or want. Very soon, then, the growing child learns to display a highly expurgated version of his self to others. I have coined the term "public self" to refer to the concept of oneself which one wants others to believe. (Jourard, 1964, p. 10)

A familiar story, especially for mothers, is that of a child running home to tell of an exciting and possibly dangerous experience. Mom is horrified at the tale and tells the child to never, never do that again. Mom's unexpected response leaves an indelible impression and the child learns one of two things: either never repeat the experience, or, if you do, don't tell Mom!

A young mother was visiting the Sunday school class of her 6-year-old daughter. The lesson was on proper behavior in church. The teacher asked the children to name places where we should not run. Lots of hands were raised and the teacher called on the children one at a time. The children offered their answers: school, the library, grocery store— but church was not mentioned. The visiting mother proudly noticed that her daughter's hand was still waving in the air, undoubtedly armed with the answer sought by the teacher. Finally, the teacher called on the daughter. With great enthusiasm, the 6-year-old responded: "The liquor store—my dad said that I should never run in the liquor store because I'll knock down the bottles." The mother was momentarily spellbound, as liquor stores were held in disrepute by this church. The child had not yet developed a "public self," at least as far as the church was concerned.

Throughout life, human beings form ideas or concepts of how they want to portray themselves. These concepts may be conditioned by the family, social networks, social or religious organizations, or employment. People tend to be selective about what they disclose about themselves. Jourard suggests:

> Our disclosures reflect, not our spontaneous feelings, thoughts and wishes, but rather pretended experience which will avoid punishment and win unearned approval. We say that we feel things we do not feel. We say that we did things we did not do. We say that we believe things we do not believe. (Jourard, 1964, p. 11)

Jourard contends that this pattern of selective disclosure, or pseudo-self-disclosure, leads to self-alienation, where "the individual loses his soul, literally." People have a greater tendency for self-disclosure when the environment is permissive and nonjudgmental. In some circumstances, people will reveal more of themselves. An experience that has occurred to a number of people is in long distance travel—particularly by bus or plane. In these experiences, people are seated in close proximity to strangers over a period of time. It is not unusual for travelers to strike up a casual conversation where they share information about themselves. In some circumstances, the travelers begin to reveal information—rather personal attitudes and feelings about work, family, or life that they might not share with acquaintances. This self-disclosure occurs for several reasons: one or both of the travelers may have sensed that they were alike, the environment is nonthreatening, and, even if one disapproved of what was heard, the travelers will likely never see each other again.

Effort is made to produce this permissive environment in focus groups. This is achieved through selection of participants, the nature of the questioning, and the establishment of focus group rules. The focus group is ideally composed of strangers—people who will likely not ever see each other again. The interviewer is not in a position of power or influence, and, in fact, encourages comments of all types—both positive and negative. The interviewer is careful not to make judgments about the responses and to control body language that might communicate approval or disapproval. At the beginning of the discussion, the interviewer purposefully sanctions and even encourages alternative explanations. For example:

> There are no right or wrong answers, but rather differing points of view. Please share your point of view even if it differs from what others have said. We are just as interested in negative comments as positive comments, and at times the negative comments are the most helpful.

Another reason why the traveling partners readily disclose is that they perceive that they are alike in some ways. It may be that they have one or more characteristics in common, such as age, sex, occupation, marital status, or hold similar attitudes on a topic of discussion. Jourard has found that individuals are selective in their self-disclosure, and the decision to reveal is based on perceptions of the other person. In his studies of self-disclosure, Jourard found that "subjects tended to disclose more about themselves to people who resembled them in various ways than to people who differ from them" (Jourard, 1964, p. 15).

Focus groups are best conducted with participants who are similar to each other, and this homogeneity is reinforced in the introduction to the group discussion. The rule for selecting focus group participants is commonality, not diversity. Care must be exercised to be alert to subtle distinctions that are not apparent to the researcher such as social status, educational level, occupational status, income, and so on. For example, one cannot assume that all clerical workers, all hospital workers, or all farmers consider themselves to be like each other. Within each category, there are distinctions that may seem subtle to the researcher but are major differences to those who are in those situations. The danger is that people tend to be hesitant to share and will defer their opinions to someone else in the group who is perceived to be more knowledgeable, wealthy, or influential. For example, a college graduate (or, heaven forbid, a Ph.D.) in a group of high school graduates, even if they have similar job responsibilities, can affect the extent of sharing. Farmers place considerable status on the number of acres they own. Regularly, farmers who own fewer acres will defer to a farmer with greater acreage. In part, this may be an unwarranted assumption that acreage, prosperity, education, or income equals knowledge and more valued opinions. In a focus group, the interviewer underscores the commonality of the group in the following manner: "We have invited people with similar experiences to share their perceptions and ideas on this topic. You were selected because you have certain things in common that are of particular interest to us."

As a society, we have a predisposition to form groups and engage in collective interactions. This tendency may well be part of a common human experience that is not bounded by cultures or time. In spite of our millennia of experience and cumulative wisdom about groups, we still struggle along regularly confused about both the purpose and the process of such interactions. Focus group interviews involve people and, from outward appearances, the technique resembles experiences that are familiar to all of us. Below this surface, however, there are a number of elements that are unique from other group experiences. The focus group interview is created to accomplish a specific purpose through a defined process. The purpose is to obtain information of a qualitative nature from a predetermined and limited number of people. The focus group provides an environment where disclosures are encouraged and nurtured, but it falls to the interviewer to bring focus to those disclosures through open-ended questions within a permissive environment. Chapter 2 provides a close-up look at that environment.

2

Focus Groups

Focus groups have evolved over the past few decades and have taken on a set of characteristics that are distinctive from other group experiences. Focus groups are useful in obtaining a particular kind of information—information that would be difficult, if not impossible, to obtain using other methodological procedures. This chapter begins with an overview of focus group characteristics and then provides examples of how decision makers have used focus group procedures. This is followed by a brief overview of qualitative and quantitative research procedures and a discussion of the advantages and disadvantages of focus groups.

CHARACTERISTICS OF FOCUS GROUPS

Focus group interviews typically have five characteristics or features. These characteristics relate to the ingredients of a focus group: (a) people, who (b) possess certain characteristics, (c) provide data (d) of a qualitative nature (e) in a focused discussion. Other types of group processes used in human services (delphic, nominal, planning, therapeutic, sensitivity, advisory, and so on) may also have one or more of these features, but not in the same combination as those of focus group interviews.

Focus Groups Involve People

Focus groups are typically composed of seven to ten people, but the size can range from as few as four to as many as twelve. The size is conditioned by two factors: it must be small enough for everyone to have opportunity to share insights and yet large enough to provide diversity of perceptions. When the group exceeds a dozen participants, there is a tendency for the group to fragment. Participants want to talk but are unable to do so because there is just not a sufficient pause in the conversation. In these situations, the only recourse is for participants to share by whispering to the people next to them. When this occurs, it is clearly a signal that the group is too big. Small groups of four to six participants afford more opportunity to share ideas, but the restricted size also results in a smaller pool of total ideas. These smaller groups— sometimes called mini-focus groups—have a distinct advantage in logistics. Groups of four to six can be easily accommodated in restaurants, private homes, and other environments where space is at a premium.

Participants Are Reasonably Homogeneous and Unfamiliar with Each Other

Focus groups are composed of people who are similar to each other. The nature of this homogeneity is determined by the purpose of the study. This similarity is a basis for recruitment, and participants are typically informed of these common factors at the beginning of the discussion. This homogeneity can be broadly or narrowly defined. For example, suppose an adult community education program wanted to know more about reaching people not now participating in their services. In this case, homogeneity is broadly defined as adults who live in the community who have not yet attended community education sessions. The group might vary by age, gender, occupation, and interest, but members have the commonality of being adults, residents, and nonusers. If, however, the community education programs are targeted for certain occupations, residents in defined geographic areas, or are offered only during certain times, then the researcher would use a narrower definition of homogeneity in selecting participants. The issue is essentially: Who do you want to hear from? The researcher should decide who the target audience is and invite people with those characteristics.

Focus groups are usually composed of people who do not know each other—ideally it is best if participants are complete strangers. In some communities, this is virtually impossible; nevertheless, close friends or those who work together shouldn't be included in the same group. Caution should be exercised when conducting focus groups within organizations; especially among people who have regular contact with each other. People who regularly interact, either socially or at work, present special difficulties for the focus group discussion because they may be responding based on known past experiences, events, or discussions. Moreover, familiarity tends to inhibit disclosure. A related, yet equally important, issue is the familiarity between the interviewer and the participants. When nonprofit organizations use focus groups, they may wish to use staff persons or even volunteers to moderate the discussion. If the staff member or volunteer is readily identified with the organization, or, for that matter, identified with any controversial issue in the community, the quality of the results could be jeopardized. For example, the top administrator of a statewide nonprofit institution was convinced that focus groups would provide valuable insights about the concerns of field staff. The administrator wanted to moderate these discussions with subordinates personally. The administrator was clearly in a hierarchical position and made the final decisions on salary, job responsibilities, and hiring and termination. In this situation, we encouraged the administrator to identify a neutral moderator outside of the organizational chain of command.

The concern about familiarity of participants is really an issue of analysis. The analyst is unable to isolate what influenced the participants. Were the findings related to the issue being discussed or could the comments have been influenced by past, present, or the possibility of future interaction with other group members?

**Focus Groups Are a
Data Collection Procedure**

Focus groups produce data of interest to researchers. In this respect, the purpose differs from other group interactions where the goal is to reach consensus, provide recommendations, or make decisions among alternatives. Delphic processes and nominal groups differ from focus groups in that they attempt to identify consensus and agreeable solutions, an important objective but considerably different from the purpose of focus groups. Brainstorming techniques resemble the freedom and spontaneity of focus groups but once again differ in that brainstorming is often directed to solving particular problems. Brainstorming, nominal groups, and delphic processes are all used primarily with people who are experts or are knowledgeable in finding potential solutions. Focus groups, however, pay attention to the perceptions of the users and consumers of solutions, products, and services. Focus groups have a rather narrow purpose for which they work particularly well—that is, to determine the perceptions, feelings, and manner of thinking of consumers about products, services, or opportunities. Focus groups are not intended to develop consensus, to arrive at an agreeable plan, or to make decisions about which course of action to take.

**Focus Groups Make Use of
Qualitative Data**

Focus groups produce qualitative data that provide insights into the attitudes, perceptions, and opinions of participants. These results are solicited through open-ended questions where respondents are able to choose the manner in which they respond and also from observations of those respondents in a group discussion. The focus group presents a natural environment where participants are influencing and influenced by others—just as they do in real life. The researcher serves several functions in the focus group: moderating, listening, observing, and eventually analyzing using an inductive process. The inductive researcher derives understanding based on the discussion as opposed to testing or confirming a preconceived hypothesis or theory.

**Focus Groups Have
a Focused Discussion**

The topics of discussion in a focus group are carefully predetermined and sequenced, based on an analysis of the situation. This analysis includes an in-depth study of the event, experience, or topic in order to describe the context of the experience and the ingredients or components of the experience. The questions are placed in an environment that is understandable and logical to the participant. The moderator uses predetermined, open-ended questions. These questions appear spontaneous but are carefully developed after considerable reflection. The questions—called the questioning route—are then arranged in a natural, logical sequence and are usually memorized by the moderator. One of the unique elements of focus groups is that there is no pressure on the moderator to have the group reach consensus. Instead attention is placed on understanding the thought processes used by participants as they consider the issues of discussion.

The term *focus group* is in such vogue that it is frequently used to apply to any group discussion experience. These group experiences may contain some or most of the characteristics of focus groups but may be deficient in other features. Recently, a large metropolitan school district conducted a series of what were called "focus groups" in order to develop a strategic plan. The "focus groups" consisted of a prominent local resident standing in front of open meetings where the entire community was invited to attend. In fact, the meetings might have been better called a community forum, a discussion, or possibly a hearing. In spite of the confusion over the focus group label, there is value in careful and selective modification of focus group procedures. Modification of the focus group may even be preferred for some applications. Chapter 10 provides an overview of some modifications of the focus group interview, including repeated focus groups, multiple moderators, focus groups within organizations, and focus groups on the telephone. When considering these and other modifications, it is of value to be aware of the traditions and the rationale that have been associated with focus group interviews. When describing the strengths of focus groups, Gerald Linda relates:

> I submit to you that there is no unanimity of goals or practice in these groups. Nor is there a uniform similarity in educational background among the moderators of these groups. The reason is that the focus group is to qualitative research what analysis of variance is to quantitative research. The technique is robust, hardy, and can be twisted a bit and still yield useful and significant results. (Linda, 1982, p. 98)

THE USES OF FOCUS GROUPS

Nonprofit organizations regularly perform services or conduct programs that touch the lives of a number of people. At times, decision makers in the organization seek to get a reading of how these activities are perceived by a variety of parties: staff, volunteers, program users, potential program users, and so on. Focus groups can be used to provide information to decision makers about these opportunities at three different points in time: before, during, or after the program or service is provided.

Focus Groups Before a Program Begins

Focus groups can be used before an experience such as in planning (including strategic planning), needs assessment, assets analysis, program design, or market research. Each of these tasks typically draws upon information from several sources, one of which is particularly suited to focus groups—the perceptions of both current and potential clientele. Here are examples of how focus groups have been used at the beginning of a program or experience.

Example 1:
Generate Information
for Questionnaires

Focus groups have provided valuable background information prior to mail-out surveys. The Minnesota Extension Service commissioned an evaluation of a farm credit mediation program, and the research team planned a large-scale mail-out survey of farmers, creditors, volunteer mediators, and county extension agents. The research team needed to obtain information that was both complex and sensitive. Some of the farmers included in the survey were on the verge of bankruptcy or foreclosure and were attempting to reach mediated settlements that would allow them to remain on the farm. By using individual and small group interviews in advance of the mail-out survey, the research team was able to develop questions that would be consistently understood and accepted by various audiences and also was able to develop successful survey procedures (Krueger, Mueller, & Casey, 1986).

Example 2:
Needs Assessment

The Minnesota State Board of Vocational Technical Education had been concerned about the declining enrollment in agricultural programs at the eight area vocational technical institutes. In an effort to assess needs, a mail-out questionnaire was sent to hundreds of farmers and agribusiness personnel. Instructors at the area institutes then used this assessment to develop new courses based on expressed needs. Even though the respondents indicated that they would attend courses, the actual attendance was extremely low. What went wrong? In the next year of the study, professor Roland Peterson and his colleagues at the University of Minnesota instituted a series of focus groups to discover what would influence attendance. The focus groups revealed important information about potential clientele. Promotional flyers of courses were informative but personal invitations were much more effective in promoting attendance. Knowledgeable and practical instructors plus relevant class experiences attracted students. Despite the depressed farm economy, farmers did not perceive course tuition as a deterrent to enrollment. When staff at the technical institutes implemented the recommendations from focus group interviews, the results were impressive. The new procedures resulted in a tenfold enrollment boost of over 1000 new farmers (Peterson & Migler, 1987).

Example 3:
Needs Assessment

Susan DeVogel (1986) conducted a series of 13 focus groups to determine needs and assess the morale of United Methodist ministers. While the clergy found satisfaction in their work, they were also afflicted with self-doubts and loneliness. DeVogel relates: "Ministers do not seem to be very successful at either ministering to themselves or finding other spiritual resources for their own growth. Spiritual hunger seems to run deep, and many expressed a need for pastoral care for themselves and their families" (DeVogel, 1986, p. 1150).

Example 4:
Test New Programs

Rhonda Lincoln, a county extension agent, recently conducted a series of focus groups to test a new program idea. The new program was designed to attract low-income homemakers who had completed a nutrition education program. As a result of the focus group discussions, the advantages and disadvantages of the new program were seen more clearly by professional staff (Lincoln, 1987).

Example 5:
Discover What Customers
Consider When Deciding

MCI entered the long-distance telephone market several years ago and began using focus groups to determine how customers made decisions relating to their phones. Focus groups yielded insights that changed policies on minimum rates, securing the business market and new advertising procedures. Customers did not blame the phone company for high long-distance rates; they blamed themselves for talking too long. As a result, MCI launched their advertising motto: "You're not talking too much, just spending too much." The strategy was successful and MCI emerged with a sizable share of the new telephone market (Kahaner, 1986).

Example 6:
Discover What Customers
Consider When Deciding

General Electric discovered in focus groups that consumers were annoyed that microwaves took up so much space in the kitchen. GE engineers were toying with the idea of over-the-range microwaves but lacked the green light from consumers. Armed with this new information, GE introduced the "Spacesaver," thereby implying that the consumer might actually save some space with this new appliance. The marketing strategy was successful, and, within a year, GE had taken over the number one spot in microwave sales (Antilla & Sender, 1982). New ideas and programs regularly require an investment of scarce resources. Focus groups are very helpful in providing decision makers with information on the acceptability and consequences of those new endeavors. When asked what was the best use of focus groups, Gordon Black, a market researcher for a Rochester, New York, firm replied: "Their best use is to help you avoid doing really dumb things" (Kelleher, 1982, p. 91). Alan Andreasen recommends focus groups as a way to provide helpful information to management prior to launching a new product:

> When a company uses several focus group sessions covering the range of people likely to be target market members for the new venture, officials can spot serious problems mentioned by a modest number of participants and abort a service or product launching. Elaborate probability sampling designs are simply not necessary to satisfy this objective. (Andreasen, 1983, p. 75)

Focus Groups During a Program

Focus groups can be conducted during a program or experience such as in customer surveys, formative evaluations, or recruiting new clientele for existing programs. Consider the following examples of how others have used focus groups while a program or activity was underway.

Example 7:
Recruiting New Clientele
to an Existing Program

Charlotte Nakamura, an extension home economist in Maui County, Hawaii, was concerned about reaching young homemakers with educational programs. The traditional homemakers' organization did not seem to appeal to these busy working women and yet they could benefit from knowledge and skills in home economics and family living. Focus groups with selected young working homemakers confirmed that this audience was generally not aware of extension home economics opportunities. Future extension programs needed to be timely, accessible, and affordable if they are to be successful. Working homemakers recommended conducting future programs at work sites. In this situation, the focus group discussions provided helpful tips for reaching new clientele (Nakamura, 1987).

Example 8:
Recruiting New Members
In an effort to reach the "unchurched," a metropolitan church conducted focus groups with people not currently attending religious services. Insights from the focus group prompted the church leaders to drop the denominational name from the church title. Baby-boomers, a target audience for the church, lacked the institutional loyalty and instead were swayed more by the quality of church programs. As a result of the focus group research, the church made changes in its name and marketing strategy to attract new participants. In this situation, the strategy proved to be very successful. Later reports indicated that the changes were so successful that the church had to position parking attendants on the church roof with walkie-talkies to direct the Sunday morning traffic (Anderson, 1986).

Example 9:
Testing Programs
That Are Underway
Hawaiian extension agents working in nutrition education were developing educational programs to promote locally grown specialty vegetable varieties. The local vegetables were high in vitamins A and C, and fiber, were lower cost, and increased local consumption would benefit the island vegetable industry. Focus groups revealed that the proposed promotional campaign in supermarkets using recipes and display posters would have very limited impact on consumer purchases of vegetables. Another promotional approach, however, would likely be much more successful. Homemakers in the focus groups indicated that food samples and in-store demonstrations were major factors that would influence new purchases. The program was modified while still in the pilot stages to use more effective procedures for vegetable promotion (Yoshino, 1987).

Focus Groups After a Program

Focus groups can be helpful after a program or event has been conducted. This might occur in assessments of programs, summative evaluations, or program postmortems to discover what went wrong. The following are examples of such uses.

Example 10:
Summative Evaluation of
a Fund-Raising Drive

Syracuse University recently launched a $100-million fund drive. The key aspect of the drive was a film depicting science and research efforts. The film was shown in over two dozen focus groups of alumni, with surprising results to University officials. Alumni simply did not like the film and instead were more attracted to supporting undergraduate humanistic education (Bennett, 1986).

Example 11:
Follow-Up to a
Mail-Out Survey

Marsha Mueller and Eugene Anderson used focus groups as a follow-up to a mail-out survey of farmers in northwestern Minnesota. In the first phase of the study, over 400 randomly selected farmers participated in a mail-out survey in an attempt to identify major problems of commercial farmers. Once problems were identified, 27 farmers were invited to share interpretations of the data in three focus group discussions. The focus groups provided rich insights relating to marketing, farm decision making, and stress. The farmers in the discussions were sophisticated learners who had clear notions of what they wanted to learn. Interaction with other farmers with similar backgrounds was highly valued in educational programs, and farmers were not tolerant of instructors who had limited background in the subject area (Mueller & Anderson, 1985).

Example 12:
Understanding an
Organization's Image

The Minnesota Zoo had been in operation for nearly a decade and zoo officials were concerned about the image they had been conveying to the public. A series of focus groups revealed that entertainment was the most powerful incentive for attendance, as contrasted to education and economic value. In addition, the focus groups identified areas needing improvement such as food service and viewing distance from animals (Cook, 1986).

Example 13:
Assessment of a Product

The University of Minnesota Alumni Association conducted a series publication, *Minnesota*. The editorial staff was impressed with the diversity of opinions and commitment to the university expressed by focus group participants. Participants in focus groups wanted to see the university as it is—and to be in touch with both the challenges and the opportunities that face the university. These insights have proven helpful in making improvements in the publication ("Now We're Group Focusing," 1986).

Example 14:
Feedback to Administrators

Focus groups with pharmacy students have been found to be a helpful feedback tool for university administrators in the School of Pharmacy at the University of North Carolina. They held focus groups to uncover the nature and extent of problems encountered by students. Diamond and Gagnon (1985, p. 54) concluded that "focus group techniques are both useful and valid for assessing student problems within undergraduate pharmacy curriculum."

QUALITATIVE AND QUANTITATIVE
RESEARCH PROCEDURES

Research is often categorized as qualitative or quantitative. The former concentrates on words and observations to express reality and attempts to describe people in natural situations. By contrast, the quantitative approach grows out of a strong academic tradition that places considerable trust in numbers that represent opinions or concepts. I have discovered through experience that information users regularly have a limited understanding of quantitative procedures and vague perceptions of qualitative techniques. As a result, I have found it helpful to provide these individuals with a brief overview of each procedure by the use of an example.

Here is an example that highlights the use of qualitative and quantitative methods. The first approach was quantitative. The purpose of the study was to determine whether or not volunteers were satisfied with their positions. All 150 volunteers were invited to complete a short questionnaire containing one key question: How satisfied are you with your volunteer position?

[ ] 5. Very Satisfied
[ ] 4. Satisfied
[ ] 3. Neither Satisfied nor Dissatisfied
[ ] 2. Dissatisfied
[ ] 1. Very Dissatisfied

The analysis revealed an average score of 4.1, which would indicate that overall the workers were satisfied. When the results were separated by work responsibilities, it was discovered that those who had served as volunteers for over three years had a lower level of satisfaction. The experienced volunteers had an average score of 1.7, which indicated a cause for concern. The survey was helpful because it provided a composite score for all volunteers and highlighted a specific group that needed greater attention.

The second approach was qualitative. The qualitative approach was to ask participants how they felt about their volunteer positions. They then used their own words as opposed to the response categories used in the quantitative questionnaire. A qualitative survey involving all volunteers would take too much time and resources, so instead 48 people were randomly selected to participate in four focus group interviews. The theme of the focus group was volunteering, and people were invited to share their views and reasons for satisfaction or dissatisfaction. Volunteers expressed their opinions in various ways, but a theme emerged. The critical factor was access to printed materials used by volunteers in their teaching. In the past year, the organization decided to save money by cutting the printing budget and restricted the amount of printed materials available to these volunteers. Those who were used to having easy access to printed materials now found themselves with fewer educational tools. As a result, the experienced volunteers were dissatisfied.

In the qualitative example, there were no percentages, but the researcher obtained an explanation of why there was dissatisfaction. The percentage of respondents indicating satisfaction versus dissatisfaction was helpful information, but in this example, the qualitative results provided decision makers with the critical information for correcting the problem. Typically, qualitative research will provide in-depth information into fewer cases whereas quantitative procedures will allow for more breadth of information across a larger number of cases.

In some situations, quantitative data can be carefully obtained using well-designed questionnaires and incorporating elaborate analysis but still be dead wrong. In his classic 1934 study, Richard LaPiere surveyed the attitudes of hotel owners in providing lodging for Chinese travelers in the United States. Overwhelmingly, the innkeepers indicated that they would not provide lodging; however, in actual practice, 54 of the 55 hotels actually had provided lodging to Chinese travelers in the previous year. In this situation, the quantitative study of attitudes provided a measurement of what the innkeeper thought he would do, but in fact, the qualitative observations of the researcher proved to be far more accurate indicators of actual behavior.

> Quantitative measurements are quantitatively accurate; qualitative evaluations are always subject to the errors of human judgment. Yet it would seem far more worth while to make a shrewd guess regarding that which is essential than to accurately measure that which is likely to prove quite irrelevant. (LaPiere, 1934, p. 237)

Qualitative data are typically welcomed by decision makers because the results are presented in a concrete and understandable manner. Unfortunately, quantitative data have a complexity that is met with suspicion. Alkin, Daillak, and White (1979, p. 237) contend that "it is a simple fact that many people are uncomfortable in dealing with quantitative data." Carol Weiss (1976, p. 226) suggests that there is good reason for the discomfort. Social scientists have aided and abetted the communication obstacles due to methodological, technical, and statistical "jargon that litters their prose." As a result, Weiss relates, the decision maker "has to either accept or reject the researcher's interpretation of the data on faith." It may well be that discomfort and lack of faith with quantitative data explain why decision makers find qualitative data to be more useful than other research (Van de Vall, Bolas, & Kang, 1976).

Increasingly, evaluation researchers are recognizing the benefits of combining qualitative and quantitative procedures, resulting in greater methodological mixes that strengthen the research design. Focus groups can be used in four different ways in relation to quantitative methods.

(1) Focus groups can precede quantitative procedures. When used in this way, the focus group interview can help the researcher learn the vocabulary and discover the thinking pattern of the target audience. In addition, focus groups can provide clues as to special problems that might develop in the quantitative phase. For example, the questionnaire might have an illogical sequence of questions that confuses respondents, might omit important response choices, or might simply fail to ask critical questions. Qualitative procedures like focus groups or individual interviews enable the researcher to get in tune with the respondent and discover how that person sees reality. These insights can then be used to develop more efficient follow-up quantitative procedures like telephone

or mail-out surveys. The quantitative studies then enable the researcher to make inferences about the larger population.

(2) Focus groups can be used at the same time as quantitative procedures. At times, the researcher may wish to use triangulation: two or more different research methods to address the same issue in order to confirm findings and to obtain both breadth and depth of information.

(3) Focus groups can follow quantitative procedures. Questionnaires typically yield a sizable amount of data, and focused interviews can provide insights about the meaning and interpretation of the results. In addition, the follow-up focus groups can suggest action strategies for problems addressed in the questionnaire. Focus groups have been particularly helpful when used after quantitative needs assessment surveys. Needs assessment surveys can be vexing to researchers because quantitative procedures alone are often incomplete. Needs assessment surveys often provide only a portion of the desired information and omit those critical factors that influence participation in a program. Furthermore, needs assessment surveys tend to identify concerns that already have achieved some visibility within the community as opposed to the less visible concerns that lie below the surface. Some of these visible needs may have already been addressed by existing organizations or institutions, and by the time the survey is completed, the needs may have already been met.

(4) Focus groups can be used alone, independent of other procedures. They are helpful when insights, perceptions, and explanations are more important than actual numbers.

Focus groups can be used before a quantitative study, during a quantitative study, after a quantitative study, or independent of other methodological procedures. The decision of using a methodological mix is often made in the planning stages at the beginning of the study. In some situations, however, the researcher may consider incorporating a quantitative study after conducting focus group interviews, especially in situations where focus groups have revealed unexpected results that need further confirmation.

The Validity of
Focus Group Results

The nub of qualitative research—and its claim to validity—lies in the intense involvement between researcher and subject. Because the moderator an challenge and probe for the most truthful responses, supporters claim, qualitative research can yield a more in-depth analysis than that produced by formal quantitative methods. (Mariampolski, 1984, p. 21)

Are focus group results valid? How much confidence can one have in focus group results? Researchers frequently encounter questions such as these from lay groups or from decision makers. I have found through experience, painful at times, that these questions can present special problems for researchers. Researchers typically have spent some time thinking about this issue and are tempted to respond using evaluation jargon and concepts that are confusing to lay audiences. I have found it helpful to explain validity in the following manner: *Focus groups are valid if they are used carefully for a problem that is suitable for focus group inquiry.* If the researcher deviates from the established procedures of focus group interviews addressed earlier in this chapter, the issue of validity should be raised. Also, if the problem does not lend itself to focus groups, then focus groups are an invalid procedure. In short, focus groups are very much like other social science measurement procedures where validity depends not only on the procedures used but also on context.

Validity is the degree to which the procedure really measures what it proposes to measure. For example, if you conducted focus groups to gain perceptions on a potential program, did the focus group procedure really provide perceptions on this program or were the results artificially developed by the interactions of group participants.

The cynic can argue that nothing is valid. Measurements or assessments of the human condition can be distorted intentionally or unintentionally. People are not always truthful, and sometimes they give answers that seem best for the situation. Other times, people hold back important information because of apprehensions or social pressure. Experts who work with small groups testify about the unpredictable nature of groups, and that group leaders or moderators can skillfully or unwittingly lead groups into decisions or consensus.

Others have an optimistic faith in measurement procedures and assume that, if a procedure has been developed by leading experts, then it must be valid. Social scientists typically go to considerable effort to ensure that they are really measuring what they propose to measure. They will pilot test the procedures under varying conditions, develop protocol on how to administer the test, and at times build in questions that check on the truthfulness of the respondent.

I recommend that decision makers consider the middle ground—have some faith in all procedures but also retain skepticism. Indeed, all data should be regarded with a healthy skepticism whether they are obtained from official documents, personal interviews, questionnaires, standardized tests, opinion polls, or focused interviews.

Validity can be assessed in several ways. The most basic level is face validity: Do the results look valid? Another type of validity is the degree to which the results are confirmed by future behaviors, experiences, or events: predictive or convergent validity.

Typically, focus groups have high face validity, which is due in large part to the believability of comments from participants. People open up in focus groups and share insights that may not be available from individual interviews, questionnaires, or other data sources. Fred Reynolds and Deborah Johnson (1978) reported on a comparison of focus group discussions with a large-scale mail-out survey. The two studies were both nationwide in scope—a mail survey of 2000 females with a 90% response rate compared to a series of 20 focus groups in 10 cities. When these two market research studies were compared, there was a 97% level of agreement, and, in the area of discrepancy, the focus group results proved to have greater predictive validity when compared to later sales data.

The decision maker, when confronted with focus group results, may find explanations that seem infinitely reasonable, explanations that have come directly from the clients and not from secondhand summaries. If anything, the face validity of focus groups may be too high. Focus group results seem so believable that decision makers may have the tendency to rush out and implement the resulting recommendations without adequate skepticism.

Generalizing Focus Group Results

Researchers have tended to describe focus group results as exploratory, illuminating, and not suitable for projection to a population. Some researchers have even included a disclaimer to that effect in the focus group report, in part to temper the decision maker's urge to rush off and implement the findings. The warnings are well intended, but often do more to confuse the decision maker regarding the degree of trust to place in focus group results. Consider the following conversation:

A Conversation with
a Decision Maker

Decision maker: "Hold it a minute, professor. I like what I hear about focus groups but there's something I just don't understand. You've told me that focus groups will give me information that is exploratory, illuminating, and enlightening. I'm the person that makes the decisions. I need to know if focus group results are good enough for me to use for making decisions? I mean, those people with the numbers tell me about some kind of margin of error, which tells me something about how confident I can be that their numbers are right. You don't give me a margin of error. You tell me I can't project to the whole group—I think you call it 'infer to the population'—with this focus group stuff. Well if your focus group stuff doesn't represent the population, who does it represent and why should I use it?"

Professor: "In all research we make assumptions. We do it when we use numbers and we also do it with focus group interviews. When we do quantitative research in social sciences—things like mail-out surveys—we make a number of assumptions and sometimes the researchers do not clearly label these as assumptions. For example, sometimes we assume that the person who was sent the survey really did in fact fill it out. Sometimes these surveys are filled out by a coworker or another member of the family. We regularly make assumptions about the nature of the questions we ask. We assume that the respondent really understands the question, interprets the questions in the same way that the researcher does, and then provides us with an honest answer. The researcher also assumes that he or she knows enough about the reality of the respondent to construct meaningful questions. Then, depending on the type of analysis, we make assumptions about the nature of the numbers (nominal, ordinal, interval, ratio), and about those not responding—regarding the degree of similarity to those who did respond. In some statistical procedures, we assume that the responses are normally distributed or that variables are related in linear manner as well as other things about the population. So you see, lots of things can influence the degree of confidence we have in the data."

Decision maker: "All right professor, what about the assumptions in focus group interviewing?"

Professor: "Well, the same is true of focus group interviews. Only here the assumptions are a bit more obvious and apparent. We've selected a small number of people—often less than 50 people and sometimes as few as 15 or 20 out of a much larger number in the population. One of the greatest advantages of focus groups—or qualitative methods in general—is that they give us information in depth. The respondent can provide additional background information about the circumstances of the answer. Further-more, the researcher is in a better position to know if the respondent really understood the questions by examining the answers to follow-up questions. While you gain in depth from focus group interviews, you also lose in breadth of information when compared to most quantitative procedures. There is a risk in using focus group data to generalize to a population because the sample is not necessarily intended to be reflective of the entire population. But the same is true of using quantitative data to generalize. In a perfect survey, our statistics would allow us to generalize, but we might have asked foolish questions to begin with; when you make inferences on bad data, you don't improve the quality of your decision."

Decision maker: "Well, can I generalize or not with focus group results?"

Professor: "My suggestion is to make cautious generalizations. If you're making really big decisions where the consequences of error are major, then by all means use a multiple set of methods. If the different methodological procedures lead you to the same conclusions, then you can move with greater confidence. At times, you might have more confidence in a small qualitative samples of a carefully executed research study than with large quantitative samples with complex statistical procedures. Your goal in focus group research is to understand reality. Due to the inductive nature of focus group research, greater attention is directed to discovering the manner and way in which respondents perceived the problem. As a result, the researcher has a clearer fix on how the issue is understood by respondents. If the focus group research has been carefully conducted and appropriately analyzed, then the user should be able to make generalizations to other respondents who possess similar characteristics."

Decision maker: "OK, now who can I generalize about?"

Professor: "That's exactly the right question. When we speak of generalizing, we need to consider about whom are you attempting to generalize. Who are you talking about? You don't select a sample of senior citizens and then generalize to people of all ages. Likewise, you don't select a sample of program users and generalize to nonusers. Now, it could be true that in both of these areas the groups are similar, but you just don't know that because you've not included other groups in your sampling strategy."

Decision maker: "Thanks, now tell me more about focus groups."

ADVANTAGES OF
FOCUS GROUP INTERVIEWS

The focus group interview offers several advantages. First, it is a socially oriented research procedure. People are social creatures who interact with others. They are influenced by the comments of others and make decisions after listening to the advice and counsel of people around them. Focus groups place people in natural, real-life situations as opposed to the controlled experimental situations typical of quantitative studies. Also, the one-to-one interviews are not able to capture the dynamic nature of this group interaction. Inhibitions often are relaxed in group situations, and the more natural environment prompts increased candor by respondents. David L. Morgan and Margaret T. Spanish elaborate:

> In essence, the strengths of focus groups come from a compromise between the strengths found in other qualitative methods. Like participant observation, they allow access to a process that qualitative researchers are often centrally interested in: interaction. Like in-depth interviewing, they allow access to the content that we are often interested in: the attitudes and experiences of our informants. As a compromise, focus groups are neither as strong as participant observation on the naturalistic observation of interaction, nor as strong as interviewing on the direct probing of informant knowledge, but they do a better job of combining these two goals than either of the other two techniques. We believe this is a useful combination, and one which, for some types of research questions, may represent the best of both worlds. (Morgan & Spanish, 1984, p. 260)

The second advantage of focus group discussions is that the format allows the moderator to probe. This flexibility to explore unanticipated issues is not possible within the more structured questioning sequences typical of mail-out surveys.

A third advantage is that focus group discussions have high face validity, as discussed earlier. The technique is easily understood and the results seem believable to those using the information. Results are not presented in complicated statistical charts but rather in lay terminology embellished with quotations from group participants.

A fourth advantage is that focus group discussions are relatively low in cost. Alan Andreasen (1983, p. 75) recommends focus groups as a cost-conscious form of market research that does not require "big bucks":

> Another low-cost approach is the commissioning of focus group interviews of 8 to 12 members of the target audience at a time. Although the results are not strictly projectable to the larger market because the groups are not randomly selected, these results do cut the cost of interviewing by a quarter or a half. Interviewers can sometimes develop richer data in the relaxed, chatty format of the focus group.

A fifth advantage is that focus groups can provide speedy results. In emergency situations, skilled moderators have been able to conduct three to four discussions, analyze the results, and prepare a report in less than a week. When compared to other means of obtaining information about behaviors and attitudes, the focus group method has a considerable advantage.

A sixth advantage is that they enable the researcher to increase the sample size of qualitative studies. Qualitative studies typically have limited sample sizes due to the time and cost constraints of individual interviewing. Focus groups enable the researcher to increase the sample size without dramatic increases in the time required of the interviewer.

LIMITATIONS OF
FOCUS GROUP INTERVIEWS

All techniques for gathering information have limitations, and focus group interviews are no exception. It is important to be aware of these limitations in deciding whether to use this technique. Among the limitations are the following:

First, the researcher has less control in the group interview as compared to the individual interview. The focus group interview allows the participants to influence and interact with each other, and, as a result, group members are able to influence the course of the discussion. This sharing of group control results in some inefficiencies such as detours in the discussion, and the raising of irrelevant issues, thus requiring the interviewer to keep the discussion focused.

Second, data are more difficult to analyze. Group interaction provides a social environment, and comments must be interpreted within that context. Care is needed to avoid lifting comments out of context and out of sequence or to come to premature conclusions. Occasionally, participants will modify or even reverse their positions after interacting with others.

Third, the technique requires carefully trained interviewers. At times, an untrained moderator can achieve remarkable results, but it is far better to influence the odds of success by using skilled interviewers. The open-ended questioning, the use of techniques like pauses and probes, and knowing when and how to move into new topic areas require a degree of expertise typically not possessed by untrained interviewers.

Fourth, groups can vary considerably. Each focus group tends to have unique characteristics. One group can be lethargic, boring, and dull; the next selected in an identical manner might be exciting, energetic, and invigorating. Because of the differences in groups, it is recommended to include enough groups to balance the idiosyncrasies of individual sessions.

Fifth, groups are difficult to assemble. The focus group requires that people take time to come to a designated place at a prescribed time to share their perceptions with others.

Sixth, the discussion must be conducted in an environment conducive to conversation. These factors often present logistical problems and may require participant incentives to participate. By contrast, an individual interview can be held in a location and at a time most convenient to the interviewee.

SUMMARY

Focus groups are special creatures in the kingdom of groups. In terms of appearances, focus groups look very much like other kinds of group experiences. On closer inspection, however, focus groups have a distinctive cluster of characteristics:

(1) focus groups involve homogeneous people in a social interaction;
(2) the purpose of focus groups is to collect qualitative data from a focused discussion; and
(3) focus groups are a qualitative approach to gathering information that is both inductive and naturalistic.

Focus groups have been found useful prior to, during, and after programs, events, or experiences. They have been helpful in assessing needs, developing plans, recruiting new clientele, finding out customer decision processes, testing new programs and ideas, improving existing programs, and in generating information for constructing questionnaires.

Focus groups are valid if they are used carefully for a problem that is suitable for focus group inquiry.

Focus groups offer several advantages, including

(1) that the technique is a socially oriented research method capturing real-life data in a social environment;
(2) it has flexibility;
(3) it has high face validity;
(4) it has speedy results; and
(5) it is low in cost.

Focus groups have limitations that affect the quality of the results. Limitations include

(1) focus groups afford the researcher less control than individual interviews;
(2) data are difficult to analyze;
(3) moderators require special skills;
(4) differences between groups can be troublesome;
(5) groups are difficult to assemble; and
(6) the discussion must be conducted in a conducive environment.

The kingdom of groups has many creatures and some of them look very much alike. The focus group is one of those experiences that resembles other group situations we may have experienced. In some respects, that is exactly what the focus group intends to do, to achieve a naturalness where people feel free to talk and share insights and observations. The way to identify the focus group is to examine the purpose and the process of the group experience, as reviewed in Chapter 1, and then consider the degree of fit with the characteristics included in this chapter.

Part II

The Process of Conducting Focus Groups

The process of conducting a focus group study consists of three phases: conceptualizing the study, conducting the interviews, and analyzing and reporting the results of the data gathered. Within each of these phases, there are steps that require consideration and action.

The conceptualization phase is critical for successful focus group interviews. In this phase, the researcher gives consideration to the purpose of the study as well as to the users of the information. The researcher then develops a plan that will guide the remainder of the research process. This conceptualization phase is discussed in Chapter 3.

The conducting phase consists of three distinct tasks, all of which must be completed prior to the first group interview. This includes developing the questions (Chapter 4), learning interviewer skills (Chapter 5), and selecting group participants (Chapter 6). The focus groups are then conducted at the conclusion of these three steps.

The analysis/reporting phase is the final aspect of the focus group process. The data are analyzed (Chapter 7), followed by reporting the results (Chapter 8).

3

Conceptualizing the Focus Group

Once upon a time, there was an adventurous little field mouse who lived in a large forest. The field mouse had rarely wandered far from home, but on one sunny summer day the urges for fame and fortune were too great to resist. "Besides," he thought, "I need to see the world." In spite of warnings from mama and papa, the little field mouse took the coins from his piggy bank, put them in his knapsack and set off to seek fame and fortune. After a short while, the field mouse met an eagle.

"Where are you going?" asked the eagle.

"I'm off to seek fame and fortune," said the field mouse.

"Well," said the eagle, "For two coins I'll sell you this feather that will speed you through the forest."

"Great," said the field mouse as he gave the coins to the eagle.

Soon the field mouse came across a squirrel.

"Where ya' headed?" inquired the squirrel.

"I plan to see the world and make my fortune," replied the little field mouse.

"Well, in that case you'll want to get there as quickly as possible. I have these special acorns that will give you extra energy and help you get there faster. Ya got any coins?" asked the squirrel.

"Sure," said the little field mouse and he swapped two coins for two acorns and hurried on his way, until he was stopped by a wolf.

"You seem to be in a big rush," said the wolf. "Where ya goin'?"

"I'm off to seek my fortune and I'm goin' as fast as I can," replied the field mouse.

"There's a shortcut that will get you there immediately," said the wolf with a toothy grin. "Just go right through that hole over there," and little field mouse dashed into the wolf's den, never to be seen again.

The moral of this tale is that, if you don't know where you're headed, you're likely to end up somewhere else—and it could cost you more than a few coins.

In one sense, conceptualizing or planning seems so simple. Unfortunately, however, human memories are imperfect, our species is not always rational or logical, and the environment in which we operate is dynamic. At times, the best laid plans go astray, and, admittedly, there are situations where sketchy plans are a roaring success. Comprehensive and rigid plans may not be worth the effort, but lack of planning is even more dangerous. The moderate and recommended approach is to find the level of planning appropriate to the situation.

Think of the plan as a small investment in time and energy that is intended to prevent costly mistakes. The plan keeps the study on target and enables the researcher to arrive at the intended destination within time and budget guidelines. The conceptualization stage involves consideration of the purpose, the users, the target audience, and matching all of these to the available resources in a written plan.

DETERMINE THE PURPOSE

Planning begins by reflecting on the purpose of the study and is followed by organizing those thoughts in a logical, sequential manner. At times, the need for the study might originate from someone relatively unfamiliar with focus group interviews. For example, a director of an educational organization might wish to reach new clientele; a curriculum coordinator might want to test out new programs; or a coordinator of county human services may want to discover perceptions of the organization. When the idea of the study is handed down to a research unit in a bureaucratic organization, there is often need for additional clarity and precision on the nature of the problem and what information is being requested. Failure to clarify the problem can result in a sizable investment of time and resources that miss the mark. To avoid this wasted time, the researcher should begin by writing down as precisely as possible a description of the problem at hand and the purposes of the study. This step is of considerable value both to beginning researchers and to experts. This background information should include a discussion of the following:

Why such a study should be conducted?

What types of information are of particular importance?

Who wants the information?

It is important to respond to these questions in writing to share the ideas with others and receive feedback from the expected users of the study. The first goal is to achieve agreement on the nature of the problem and the types of information needed to address the problem. Organizational politics, incomplete disclosure, and hidden agendas are among the obstacles encountered in achieving agreement, therefore, open and written communication by the researcher is often essential for further progress.

When this agreement is achieved, the next step is to consider what research procedures are appropriate. Up to this point, the research procedures have not yet been identified, and this process of determining the purpose is essential no matter what methods are used for obtaining information. It is at this point that the researcher begins to think about the benefits of alternative information sources such as surveys, observation, individual interviews, focus groups, or a combination of several procedures. Before launching a focus group study, it may be helpful to review the advantages and disadvantages of focus groups contained in Chapter 2.

Another important beginning step in the focus group technique is to consider the information needs of intended users. Involve those individuals who have a vested interest, or stake, in the study. This step has three components:

(1) Identify who will use the information.
(2) Determine what information is needed.
(3) Know why the information is needed.

The decision makers in the organization will likely be primary users, but there are other users or decision makers as well. Volunteers and advisory groups could be involved in making decisions on the future of the program. The researcher should spend time with the information users—to get to know them and listen to their concerns. Later reports will be written or presented to these people. Think of them as individuals and not as a group or category of people. Also keep in mind that there may be multiple users and the researcher will need to allocate some time to get in touch with each user.

Those who make decisions on the adoption of programs may not know what information is essential. You've probably heard it before: "I don't know what I'm looking for, but I'll know it when I see it." These experiences occur with regularity and the researcher needs to probe the issue a little deeper or risk missing the mark completely. In these situations, a helpful strategy is asking the decision maker to describe the end result or how the results will be used. Occasionally, the client can envision characteristics of the final result, and if these are described, the researcher can then design a process to collect this information. A variation of the strategy is to ask the decision makers to think out loud about how they will make decisions regarding the program. Listen for the type and nature of evidence they feel they need as they ponder the program's future.

Information is sought for a variety of reasons. In some situations, the information might be used for a specific and defined decision at a designated point in time. In other situations, the information might merely provide interested parties with insights on the nature of the program and participants. At times, the information is sought because of tradition or a perceived expectation from others in the environment. As a result, the researcher must inquire about the "why" of the study and then become an active listener. I have found it beneficial to ask the question of why the information is needed in several different ways. For example: "Tell me about the background of the proposed study." "What prompted you to consider the study?" "Who is interested in the study results?" "What might those individuals do with the study results?" This pattern of questioning can enable the researcher to get a better picture of the information needs of intended users and thereby keep the study on target.

DETERMINE WHOM TO STUDY

The researcher should consider the purpose of the study and think about who can provide the information. The researcher should attempt to be as specific as possible in this endeavor. For example, suppose decision makers were interested in how clients perceive current programs. On the surface, this question appears straightforward, but it may be complex and require more thought. Are the decision makers interested in current clientele, past clientele, or potential clientele? Precise definition of the clientele is essential to undertaking the study.

Nonprofit organizations often have a variety of educational or service-related programs. Some of the programs may be more intensive, visible, or popular than others. The researcher should give thought to both the diversity of people who participate in programs as well as their exposure to the variety of program opportunities. Nonprofit and service organizations typically have three categories of people who are of special importance: advisory groups, employees, and clients. Each of these three audiences could represent an area of study with focus group interviews. Information could be provided by

(1) Advisory groups—the organizational decision makers

    (a) advisory boards with budgetary authority
    (b) advisory committees in subject areas

(2) Employees

    (a) employees who deliver programs and services
    (b) support staff who perform clerical and related functions
    (c) administrators and managers

(3) Customers or clients

    (a) clients who use the program—limited, moderate, or heavy users
    (b) potential clients who are not currently using the programs or services

In addition, consideration should be given to the more traditional ways of dividing people into categories. Factors such as geographic location, age, gender, income, participation characteristics, family size, and employment status are all helpful ways to identify who should participate in focus groups. The decision of whom to involve must be related to the purpose of the study. These demographic factors will be important in determining who should be invited to the focus group interviews.

DEVELOP A PLAN AND
ESTIMATE RESOURCES NEEDED

The researcher should begin by a writing description of the problem and a plan of action. This plan should include the procedures that will be followed, whether a task force will be involved, a time line, and a proposed budget. The value of the written plan is threefold. First, it forces the researcher to think through the steps in a logical manner. Ideas that seem to make sense in our heads sometimes have easily

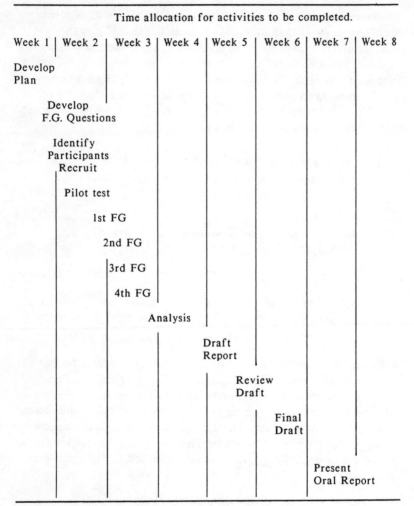

Figure 3.1: Chronological Plan

identifiable shortcomings when placed on paper. Second, the written plan allows more effective feedback from decision makers. Written plans can be circulated, distributed, and discussed more readily than our invisible thoughts. Third, it ensures that adequate resources and time are available to obtain needed information.

The plan should be shared with colleagues, particularly those who have assisted in developing the program. It is also helpful to share it with

Task	Person responsible	Days Needed	Budget	Comments
Planning	Dick	2		
Develop Questions	Dick	1		Dick leads
	Task force of 4 people .2 x 4 =	.8		brainstorming
	Marsha	.5		with task force
Identify Participants	Dick	.5		
Feedback on Plan/pilot test with task force	Dick	.5		
	Task force of 4 people .2 x 4 =	.8		
Obtain list of potential participants	Dick	.5		From
	County office managers .2 x 4 =	.8		county offices
Recruitment	Secretary (2 calls, 1 letter)	8	$200	Phone calls
	Dick supervises	.5		& letters
4 Focus Groups	Dick moderates	3	$120 Room	
	Marsha assists	3	$80 Refreshments	
			$160 Travel	
Type 4 FG Transcripts	Secretary	5	$50 Supplies	
Analysis	Dick	4		
	Marsha	1		
Type Draft Report	Secretary	1	$20 Supplies	
			$20 Copies	
Review Draft	Task force .2 x 4 =	.8		
Revision	Dick	.5		
	Secretary	.5		
Printing	Secretary	.2	$200 Printing	
Present Report	Dick	1		

TOTALS: Time Dick=13.5 days, Marsha=4.5 days, Task Force=2.4 days, Sect=14.7days
Office managers=.8 day.
Budget $560

Figure 3.2: Fiscal Plan

colleagues or professionals familiar with focus group interviewing procedures. When others are asked to review the plan, they should be requested to identify aspects that are illogical, impractical, or unclear. Feedback that spots these problems early in the planning is most helpful and should be encouraged. It may be of value to also share these plans with those who are making decisions on the program. These decision makers could be invited to comment on whether critical information is overlooked.

The effective plan should contain information on the chronological sequence of events, due dates, costs involved, and decision points where the plan may be modified or abridged. Consideration should be given to developing both a *chronological plan* and a *fiscal plan* for the project.

A chronological plan should contain the following elements: dates, steps, persons responsible, people assisting, and comments. The chronological plan presents a timetable of the sequence of steps as well as identifying the tasks to be completed by various individuals. Administrators have regularly criticized evaluators and researchers for not respecting the time requirements of decision making. At some point, a decision will be made, regardless of whether or not the results are available. The chronological plan provides decision makers with a timetable for information—a timetable that must be prepared in advance and then respected by both the researcher and the decision maker.

The fiscal plan is a project budget summary that complements the chronological plan and provides additional insights as to the amount of time, effort, and expenses that will be required. It is often helpful to consider both the high and low estimates of all needed resources.

SUMMARY

The written description of purpose comes first. This is followed by identification of the questions or issues to be studied and the target audience that will provide the answers. The written plan is a road map to achieving a successful design. This task of writing assists in organizing and it allows other significant partners to provide helpful feedback. Focus groups require resources: time and money. Sound conceptualization and planning ensures appropriate questions and allocation of adequate resources.

4

Asking Questions in a Focus Group

The mother thought her daughter should have a comprehensive checkup before starting kindergarten. To be on the safe side, she made an appointment with an eminent psychologist to examine the youngster for any possible abnormal tendencies. Among the questions, the man of science asked: "Are you a boy or a girl?" "A boy," the little girl answered. Somewhat startled, the psychologist tried again. "When you grow up, are you going to be a woman or a man?" "A man," the little girl answered. On the way home, the mother asked, "Why did you make such strange replies to what the psychologist asked you?" In a serious tone of voice, the little girl replied, "Since he asked such silly questions, I thought he wanted silly answers!"

Quality answers are directly related to quality questions. Forethought must be given to developing questions for a focus group. Questions are the heart of the focus group interview. These questions appear to be spontaneous, but have been carefully selected and phrased in advance to elicit the maximum amount of information. We tend to be too casual about asking questions. We're exposed to questions every day and perhaps it is this continuous exposure that has dulled our senses to the importance of asking quality questions. In order to understand the features of a quality question, we must explore some of the dynamics of communication as well as the human cognitive process.

The series of questions used in a focused interview or questioning route look deceptively simple. Indeed, novice interviewers tend to include far too many questions in the questioning route. Regularly, a focused interview will include less than ten questions and often around five or six total. If these questions were asked in an individual interview, the respondent could probably tell you everything known about the questions in just a few minutes. When these questions are placed in a group environment, however, the discussion can last for several hours. Part of the reason is in the nature of the questions and the cognitive processes of humans. As participants answer questions, the responses spark new ideas or connections from other participants. Answers provide mental cues that unlock perceptions of other participants—cues that are necessary in order to explore the range of perceptions.

THE ART OF ASKING QUESTIONS

Asking quality questions is not easy, it requires forethought, concentration, and some background knowledge. Consider the following characteristics of good questions for focus groups.

Focus Group Interviews Use Open-Ended Questions

Open-ended questions allow the respondent to determine the direction of the response. These open-ended questions provide an opportunity for the respondent to answer from a variety of dimensions. The answer is not implied and the type or manner of response is not suggested. Individuals are encouraged to respond based on their specific situation. These open-ended questions are particularly appropriate in the beginning of the focused interview, but they can be effectively used throughout the discussion. The major advantage of the open-ended question is that it reveals what is on the interviewee's mind as opposed to what the interviewer suspects is on the interviewee's mind. Toward the end of the group interview, it is often productive to limit the types of responses and bring greater focus to the answers by shifting to closed-ended questions.

The questions are the "stimulus" for the respondent. This stimulus can be of two varieties: structured or free. If the stimulus is free, as in an open-ended question, it allows the respondent the opportunity to structure an answer in any of several dimensions. Merton et al. (1956, p. 15) describe this type of question as "one which does not fix attention on any specific aspect of the stimulus situation or of the response, it is, so to speak, a blank page to be filled in by the interviewee." Consider the following examples of open-ended questions:

"What did you think of the program?"

"How did you feel about the conference?"

"Where do you get new information?"

"What do you like best about the proposed program?"

It is possible to add structure to the stimulus question by delimiting or bounding the question and yet allowing respondents to select their own way of answering. For example:

"What did you think of the part of the program that described new farming techniques?"

"How did you feel about Dr. Jones's presentation at the conference?"

"Where do you get new information on parenting skills?"

"What do you like best about how the new program is promoted?"

Some questions are deceptive and appear to be open-ended, but are really closed-ended questions in disguise. Questions that include words and phrases like *satisfied, to what extent,* or *how much* imply answers that fall within a specified range such as *very satisfied, to a great extent,* or *a great deal.* These questions are usually preferred toward the latter parts of the focused interview as the moderator narrows the range of inquiry. Bounding the questions in this manner may also be helpful to the moderator in an effort to regain control of a rambling discussion or in situations where the topic requires more specific insights to the topic of discussion.

Focus Group Interviews Avoid Dichotomous Questions

Dichotomous questions are those that can be answered with a simple "yes" or "no" response. These questions are often asked in social situations, and part of our socialization is the ability to sense what the question really means and answer accordingly. "Did you have a nice day?" "Do you feel OK?" "It's a nice party, isn't it?" or "Do you work at the university?" can be answered literally with a "yes" or "no" or expanded upon.

It is interesting to note that children, and particularly teenagers, answer questions literally, especially questions from parents. Consider the conversation described by Patton:

(Teenager returns home from a date.)

Oh, you're home a bit late?

Yeah.

Did you have a good time?

Yeah.

Did you go to a movie?

Yeah.

Was it a good movie?

Yeah, it was OK.

So, it was worth seeing?

Yeah, it was worth seeing.

I've heard a lot about it. Do you think I would like it?

I don't know. Maybe.

Anything else you'd like to tell me about your evening?

No, I guess that's it.

(Teenager goes upstairs to bed. One parent turns to the other and says: It sure is hard to get him to talk to us. I guess he's at that age where kids just don't want to tell their parents anything.) (Patton, 1980, pp. 212-214)

Dichotomous questions seem appealing because they are so simple, easy to ask, and familiar in social situations. Researchers should use them with caution, however. In focus group interviews, the yes-no question usually does not evoke the desired group discussion. They also tend to elicit ambiguous responses, which can in turn restrict the clarity of the discussion.

"Why" Is Rarely Asked in a Focus Group

Why questions imply a rational answer, one developed by thought and reflection. A great many decisions are made by impulse, by habit or tradition, or generally in a nonrational manner. When asked why, respondents provide quick answers that seem rational or appropriate to the situation. Moreover, the why question has a sharpness or pointedness to it that reminds one of interrogations. This sharpness sets off defensive barriers and the respondent tends to take a position on the socially acceptable side of controversial issues.

If the researcher decided to use a why question, it should be specific. Paul Lazarfeld (1986) has referred to this as the principle of specification. Lazarfeld's principle of specification is that why questions typically can be answered on two levels. When asked why, the respondent may respond on (a) the basis of "influences" that prompted the action, or (b) the basis of certain desirable "attributes."

Lazarfeld's model can then be used to examine the responses to a seemingly simple question: "Why did you go to the zoo?"

Influence Answer: "Because my kids really wanted to go."

Attribute Answer: "Because I wanted to see the Beluga whale."

What seems like a straightforward and simple question can really be answered on several dimensions. The first answer describes an influence and the second answer relates to a feature or attribute of the zoo. The preferred strategy is to break the why question down into different questions, for example:

Influence: "What prompted (influenced, caused, made) you to go to the zoo?"

or,

Attribute: "What features of the zoo do you particularly like?"

A less directive approach is to ask people "what" or "how" they feel about the object of discussion. Often people are able to describe the feelings they had when they considered using a particular product or program. In addition, they may be able to describe the anticipated consequences from using the product or program. Grossman (1979, p. 10) offers a succinct summary of the limits of "Why?":

In short, people can tell you what they fear and how this fear developed, which, in effect, tells you why they feel as they do. But, when they're asked "Why?" directly, it frequently creates difficulties.

Focus Group Questions Are Carefully Prepared

Good focus group questions require effort and systematic development. The best questions rarely come like a bolt of lightening out of the sky. Quality questions require reflection and feedback from others. Researchers shouldn't expect perfect questions in the early drafts, but should instead allow ample time to explore phrasing and words that achieve clarity, precision, and brevity.

The first step is to identify potential questions. The researcher begins by thinking about the problem or area of concern and listing all questions that are of interest to the users. Brainstorming sessions with information users or colleagues can be helpful in obtaining a range of possible questions and variations in phrasing. The brainstorming should begin by being as exhaustive as possible and should include all questions of interest, even if they appear to be only variations of each other. When the list is complete and no further suggestions can be made, the critical questions can be highlighted. These are the questions that capture the intent of the study.

THE ART OF
FOCUSING QUESTIONS

Focus group interviewing is more than asking questions in a group; it involves asking well-thought-out questions in a focused environment. Consider these characteristics of focusing questions.

Focus Begins with Consistent and Sufficient Background Information

Provide consistent background information to each participant about the purpose of the study to minimize tacit assumptions. In all interview situations, respondents make assumptions about the nature of the questions and then answer accordingly. These tacit assumptions are vexing because the respondent may be providing an answer but basing it on faulty assumptions. Paul Lazarfeld provides an illustration of tacit assumption from a detective story of G. K. Chesterton.

> Have you ever noticed this—that people never answer what you say? They answer what you mean—or what they think you mean. Suppose one lady says to another in a country house, "Is anybody staying with you?" the lady doesn't answer "Yes; the butler, the three footmen, the parlourmaid, and so on," though the parlourmaid may be in the room, or the butler behind her chair. She says "There is *nobody* staying with us," meaning nobody of the sort you mean. But suppose a doctor inquiring into an epidemic asks, "Who is staying in the house?" then the lady will remember the butler, the parlourmaid, and the rest. All language is used like that; you never get a question answered literally, even when you get it answered truly. (Chesterton, 1951, p. 98)

All information given in preparation for the discussion helps develop the tacit knowledge of participants. Care must be taken in all advance communication to ensure uniformity, consistency, and sufficient generality regarding the purposes of the discussion.

Focus group participants usually want to know the purpose of the session in advance. They'll ask why the session is being held, who's the sponsor, or how the information is going to be used. Answers to these questions provide clues to respondents about how or in what manner they might respond. When possible, these questions should be answered. Avoiding the answer causes undue suspicion. Answers, however, need to be couched in general and neutral terms. For example:

"We are inviting people to share their ideas and opinions on community education."

"We are interested in how homemakers get information."

There is no need to provide the respondent with details of the study at the beginning of the discussion. If the respondent is overly curious, you might indicate that "I'll be covering that at the end of our session."

Focus Questions Are Presented in a Context

It is vital to establish the context of the question so that participants are mentally ready to respond. This is accomplished by introductory comments by the interviewer and also by the first few questions in the group interview. Often, verbal cues are helpful to guide the interviewee back to the original situation, event, or experience. By using past tense and requesting the participants to "think back," the interviewer places individuals back in the original environment as opposed to the immediate interviewing situation. There is a tendency for participants to respond to the more immediate interviewing experience—the here and now—unless they are requested to shift themselves to another time frame. This focus on the past increases the reliability of the responses because it asks about specific past experiences as opposed to current intentions or future possibilities. The question asks what the person has actually done as opposed to what might be done in the future. The shift is from what might be, or ought to be, to what has been. In addition, this time shift cues the respondent to speak from actual experiences as opposed to wishes and intentions.

Occasionally, a short written questionnaire at the beginning of a group interview can effectively focus attention on the topic. For example, participants might be requested to list the positive features of the last educational meeting they attended, or identify three things they would like changed in the organization. These tactics help the participants begin thinking about the general nature of the problem and enable them to collect their thoughts.

Focus Questions Are Focused

Arrange questions in a focused sequence that seems logical to participants, but not necessarily to the evaluation researcher. The most common procedure is to go from general to specific—that is, beginning with general overview questions that funnel into more specific questions of critical interest. Avoid hitting the participants with a specific question without first establishing the context created by the more general questions.

For example, suppose that a series of focus group interviews will be held with young people. The purpose is to determine their perceptions of youth organizations and eventually to identify an effective means of advertising a particular organization. It would be premature to begin with questions on advertising the organization. Instead, the moderator might ask the participants to describe their favorite youth organization or to describe what they like about youth clubs. Later in the discussion, the moderator might narrow the topic to focus on the specific youth organization under investigation. Perhaps toward the end of the discussion, the moderator might solicit their opinions on several different approaches that are being considered for advertising the youth group.

An actual illustration of the general to specific technique of focusing questions comes from Hawaii. In an effort to gain insights into how consumers use Kona coffee, the moderator began with questions about gourmet foods, then asked about gourmet beverages. When one of the participants suggested Kona coffee, the moderator then encouraged discussion of how and when this type of coffee was used.

Serendipitous Questions

Occasionally, in the flow of a focus group interview, the moderator or assistant moderator will discover a question that might be useful to the study. The question may never have occurred to the research team prior to the discussion, but the idea is cued by comments or perceptions of participants. These serendipitous questions can be beneficial. Often, it is best to hold back on them until the end of the discussion, because they may take the discussion off on a quite different trail of unknown consequences. Also, throughout the focus group, the moderator must monitor the time remaining—without noticeably looking at the clock or watch. Unanticipated questions inserted in the middle of the discussion can take precious minutes in a potentially unproductive route. Therefore, it is best to use the final five to ten minutes for serendipitous questions.

Pilot Testing the
Focus Group Interview

Focus group interviews cannot be pilot tested in the manner used in mail-out or telephone surveys. In questionnaires, we typically select a small number of people out of the intended audience and ask them to complete the survey. In focus groups, the pilot testing must take into consideration not only the nature of the questions but the characteristics of the audience, the interactions between participants, and the moderator procedures. The pilot testing can be accomplished in several steps, beginning with having experts review the questioning route and potential probes. It is preferable that these experts have had experience with focus groups, but at a minimum they should be familiar with the purpose of the study and also be familiar with the type of participants involved in the study. In this initial pilot test, attention is placed on the logical and sequential flow of questions and on the ability of probes to elicit the information desired.

The second pilot test procedure is actually the first focus group interview. After the first focus group, the moderator should reflect once again on the wording and sequencing of the questions. Consideration should also be given to the room arrangement, the composition of the participants, and the moderator procedures in encouraging (but not directing) the participant responses.

If major changes are made in the questions or moderator procedures, then the results of the first discussion are set aside and not used in later analysis. If there are no major changes, however, the first "pilot" discussion is included in later analysis.

A final procedure that can be used in pilot testing is to seek comments from participants at the conclusion of the first group discussion. The moderator might turn off the tape recorder and indicate that the session is now concluded, but invite suggestions for upcoming group discussions.

SUMMARY

Much of the success of the focus group depends on the quality of the questions. Quality questions require forethought and planning. Successful focus groups begin with well-thought-out questions that are appropriately sequenced. Open-ended questions allow the respondent to determine the nature of the answer. Dichotomous questions and "why" questions are to be avoided. Interviews are focused by providing participants with consistent and sufficient background information and by presenting the questions in a context.

APPENDIX:
EXAMPLES OF QUESTIONING ROUTES

Example 1: A Community Service Organization— Regaining Vanishing Support

Over the past few years, a neighborhood community center has experienced a steady decline in social, athletic, and educational programs. The decline has resulted in a reduction of user fees and now the financial future of the organization is in jeopardy. Focus groups were conducted with community residents to identify areas needing improvement that might restore local participation.

Questioning route for adult family members who are not now participating in community center activities:

(1) Tell us about your favorite family leisure activity here in the community.
(2) Describe the last time you participated in leisure activities with your family here in the community.
(3) Some of you mentioned activities that were coordinated by a community organization. One of the organizations is the community center. What comes to mind as you think about the community center?
(4) If you could change one thing about the community center, what would it be?
(5) Think back to the last time you volunteered time or money to an organization. What were you thinking at the time that led you to choose this particular organization?

Example 2:
Farmers' Perceptions Regarding
Local Extension Programs

Some farmers have expressed frustration with the speed and quality of agricultural information provided by county agricultural agents. Focus groups were conducted to discover ways to improve the delivery of information to farmers.

Questioning route for farmers:

(1) Let's talk about sources of information here in the community. Where do you go for information about farming?
(2) What were your impressions of these sources of information?

> Probes: Is the information timely?
> Is it accurate or biased?
> Is it practical and useful?

(3) How does the extension service compare to other sources of information about farming?

(4) Think back to the last time you received information from the county extension service. How did you feel about the information you received?

(5) What can or should the county extension service do to provide better quality information?

(6) What can or should the county extension service do to provide information to more farmers?

Example 3:
Rural Economic Development Needs of Small Businesses

The state has recently allocated resources to promote rural economic development. Educational organizations in the state have been encouraged to develop plans for training programs for owners and managers of small businesses in the rural areas. The training programs must focus on the areas deemed important to the rural business community and also present these programs in an appealing manner. In an effort to discover preferences and to provide insights into workable opportunities, a consortium of educational organizations decided to conduct a series of focus groups.

Questioning route for owners and managers of small rural businesses:

(1) Think back to the last few weeks. Did you have an experience where you needed information? Describe that experience and tell us where you went for the information.

(2) Think back to the past year. Jot down on a piece of paper situations where you needed help. We'll take just a few minutes for you to write these down.

(3) Here is a list of topics that have been suggested for possible future programs for owners and operators of small businesses. Take a look at this list and compare it to the list you developed. Which items are the most important to you from either of the lists? (Possibly go around the group and ask each participant to respond.)

(4) What makes the area of ———————— so important to you?

(5) An item that was mentioned frequently was ———————— Where would you go to get this information?

(6) If this information were available from several places and in different forms, how would you most prefer to receive it?

Probe: one to one, phone call, newsletter, meeting, workshop, bulletin

(7) What makes the provider of the information credible or believable to you? How do you know if you can trust the information you receive?

Example 4:
A Strategic Plan for a State Cooperative Extension Service

A state Cooperative Extension Service undertook the task of developing a strategic plan. One of the sources of information needed for the plan was state residents. In this situation, the planners decided to use focus groups to obtain insights from both traditional clientele as well as those who had not recently participated in extension programs or activities.

Questioning route with local community residents:

(1) Think back to the last time you needed to get information to solve a problem. What was the problem and where did you go for information?

(2) To what extent do you see the Cooperative Extension Service as a source of information?

(3) I'd like each of you to take a few moments and fill out this list. (Pass out page.) I've listed several categories of problems or issues that may affect you and others in your community. The categories include the following: work/business, family, leisure, community, and environment. Take a moment and jot down what you think to be the most important issues in each of these categories.

(4) Which of the issues that you mentioned on your list could be solved or lessened by education or information?

Example 5:
Educational Opportunities
for Working Women

The county extension agent responsible for home economics was concerned about how working women, especially those with children, obtained needed information about home economics and family living topics. These women were not participating in any traditional extension programs.

Questioning route for working women:

(1) How do you divide up responsibilities in the home? Briefly tell us about your role and that of other family members.

(2) When you need information about something to do with the family, where do you go?

    Probes: . . . in the area of nutrition
            . . . in the area of family relations or family living
            . . . in the area of family finances

(3) How do you determine if the information you receive is sound?

(4) Some of you have mentioned that you received information from classes or workshops. Do you prefer getting information in organized group sessions or by individual contacts?

    Probe: What are the benefits of group sessions?
            What are the benefits of individual contacts?

(5) Someone mentioned opportunities available from the County Extension Service. How do these opportunities compare to others in the community?

    Probe: What are the strengths of extension educational opportunities?
            What are the weaknesses of extension educational opportunities?

Example 6:
Farmer Enrollment at
Area Technical Institutes

The Area Technical Institutes had experienced sizable enrollment declines in agricultural courses, as mentioned in Chapter 2. These rural technical institutes had traditionally recruited recent high school graduates. Because of depressing conditions in farming, however, young people were turning to nonagricultural vocations. Consequently, the technical institutes were attempting to attract midcareer farmers who might benefit from agricultural courses. A needs assessment survey of farmers had indicated that farmers perceived they had a number of educational needs, but when the technical institute offered courses on these topics, the farmers still did not attend. Focus groups were conducted to discover what it would take to get farmers to attend these courses.

Questioning route for farmers:

(1) Let's get better acquainted. Tell us where you live and the type of crops and livestock in your enterprise.

(2) Thinking back over the past months, what changes have you made in your farming operation?

(Follow-up: When you made changes where did you get the information?)

(3) The Area Vocational Institute is now offering courses for farmers. In the past year, we asked hundreds of farmers what they wanted. They told us, but when we offered the courses, the farmers didn't attend. What might be the reasons for farmers not attending?

Probe: Think back to last winter. What would have prevented you from attending one of the courses?

(4) Take a look at these outlines for the courses. What would it take to get you to attend one of these courses?

Probe: What needs to be done to get people like yourself to attend?

(5) How do you feel about

   (a) the cost of tuition? (about $1.00 per hour or $20 per course)
   (b) the location of the course?
   (c) the time of day or month of the course?
   (d) the instructors?

(6) Do you have any final thoughts on encouraging farmers to attend?

5

Moderating Skills

Interviewing looks deceptively simple but requires mental discipline, preparation, and group interaction skills. Much of the success of the focused interview depends on well-developed questions asked of the right respondents, but one more ingredient is essential—a skillful moderator.

Throughout this chapter, I have purposely opted to describe the interviewer's role by using the term *moderator*. This term highlights a specific function of the interviewer—that of moderating or guiding the discussion. The term *interviewer* tends to convey a more limited impression of two-way communication between an interviewer and an interviewee. By contrast, the focus group affords the opportunity for multiple interactions not only between the interviewer and the respondent but among all participants in the group. The focus group is not a collection of simultaneous individual interviews but rather a group discussion where the conversation flows due to the nurturing of the moderator.

SELECTING THE RIGHT MODERATOR

When selecting a moderator, it is important to look for certain personal characteristics that have particular relevance for focus group leaders. These attributes have a direct bearing on the nature of the group interaction and thereby affect the quality of discussion. The moderator should be comfortable and familiar with group processes. Previous experience in working with groups or training in group dynamics is very helpful. Amy Andrews expands on this requirement:

Since half of the moderator's function is to stimulate and guide the group, a knowledge of group dynamics would seem to be an important criterion for selection. For example, the moderator must know how to deal with a quiet, passive group, an overly exuberant group, an outspoken group member, a group member who is unqualified, a group which consistently goes off on a tangent, a group which appears to be giving inconsistent responses, a group which does not understand the question, a group which misses the point completely, a group which is inarticulate, a hostile group or group member, a nervous, tense group discussing a sensitive subject, etc. (Andrews, 1977, p. 128)

The moderator exercises a mild, unobtrusive control over the group. The discussion remains on track and, when irrelevant topics are introduced by participants, the moderator carefully and subtly guides the conversation back on target. Part of the skill of moderating is the ability of the moderator to make these transitions and yet maintain group enthusiasm and interest for the topic. The moderator also must have a sense of timing—timing for the mood of the group and the appropriateness of discussion alternatives. Like the actor who takes too many bows, the moderator also must know when to wrap up the questioning and move on to the next issue, but not prematurely.

In addition, the moderator must be a good listener, a quality that comes naturally for some people and requires considerable discipline for others. Myril Axelrod underscores the importance of listening:

> In selecting the moderator the primary requirement is how well that person is going to be able to listen—is he or she someone who is really interested in people, who want to hear what someone else has to say, who can readily establish rapport and gain the confidence of people, who can make them feel relaxed and anxious to talk? This can only happen if the moderator is genuinely that kind of person. (Axelrod, 1975b, p. 6)

The moderator must have adequate background knowledge on the topic of discussion to place all comments in perspective and follow-up on critical areas of concern. Some successful moderators are able to use naïveté to an advantage by prompting participants to amplify their comments, but if used in excess, it can become tiresome and inhibit complicated responses.

The moderator must be able to communicate clearly and precisely both in writing and orally. Complicated questions reflecting fuzzy thinking are confusing.

It is important that the moderator appear like the participants in dress and appearance. Some focus group experts are cautious about having women moderators for sessions with men and vice versa. Axelrod elaborates:

I never have women doing sessions with men because I think that men don't talk to a woman in the same way they would talk to a man or in the way they talk when they are among themselves. What we want to know is what they say when they are "talking to the fellas," not what they say because that is going to please or impress the woman moderator. (Axelrod, 1975b, p. 7)

Axelrod's cautionary note is particularly appropriate in situations where participants are relating to products that affect appearance or dress, decisions that have a direct bearing on the opposite sex, decisions that are typically made by one sex, or products or services that are primarily used by one sex.

Finally, a sense of humor is a valuable asset. Judith Langer contends that humor is one of the characteristics of a good qualitative researcher:

I don't mean telling canned jokes but finding latent humor possibilities in ordinary situations. This quality, more important than it may seem, is strongly related to imagination, creativity, and spontaneity, all needed in qualitative research. (Langer, 1978, p. 10)

THE MODERATOR AND
ASSISTANT MODERATOR

Consider using a moderator team: a moderator and an assistant moderator. With this team approach, each individual has certain tasks to perform. The moderator is primarily concerned with directing the discussion, keeping the conversation flowing, and taking minimal notes. The notes of the moderator are not so much to capture the total interview, but rather to identify future questions that need to be asked. The assistant, on the other hand, takes comprehensive notes, operates the tape recorder, handles the environmental conditions and logistics (refreshments, lighting, seating, and so on), and responds to unexpected interruptions. In addition, the assistant notes the participants' body language throughout the discussion. Occasionally, the assistant will ask additional questions near the end of the discussion or probe the response of a participant in more depth. The assistant is also extremely helpful in performing the postmeeting analysis of the session.

The assistant moderator is not usually used in private sector market research projects unless as an apprentice in training. This limited use of assistant moderators is due to additional labor costs. I have found assistant moderators well worth the investment. A second set of eyes and ears increases both the total accumulation of information and the validity of the analysis. Furthermore, an assistant provides a means for dealing with distracting interruptions to the focus group interview such as latecomers, unwanted background music, or switching tapes.

MENTAL PREPARATION

Moderators must be mentally alert and free from distractions, anxieties, or pressures that would limit their ability to think quickly on their feet. Moderating a group discussion requires concentration and careful listening. Thus they should plan their schedule to minimize the risk of unexpected pressures that would limit their ability to concentrate. They must be able to give their full attention to the group.

Moderators should practice the discipline of listening to others in group situations. Begin by focusing complete attention on a group conversation and then attempt to remember the points and views expressed by various individuals. A number of people have never learned the self-discipline of keeping silent, and for them this exercise can be torment. Effective moderating in a focus group demands that the leader avoid expressing personal points of view.

The questioning route should be memorized. Typically, the key questions will be limited to about six to ten questions, with possible subpoints within each question. The moderator will have a list of questions but will use it only as a reminder of upcoming questions. A mastery of all questions is valuable because the sequence of questions is sometimes modified during the interview. Glancing at the questioning route to remember the next question is tolerable, but reading the question (and taking eyes off the participants) destroys the spontaneous flow of the discussion.

Another aspect of mental preparation is the discipline of listening and thinking simultaneously. It is not enough to be an empty vessel, listening and absorbing the comments of participants. Judith Langer offers a series of questions that pass through the moderator's mind while the discussion is in process:

—What else do I need to ask to understand this respondent's statement— what it means, why he/she feels that way, etc.?

—Am I hearing everything I need to know to understand the problem and answer the objectives of the research? Is there a question not on the topic guide [questioning route] that I should ask?

—How much time do I have left? Will I be able to cover everything when just one section of the topic guide could take the full two hours?

—What does all this mean anyway? What am I learning about consumer feelings, beliefs, and behavior? What ideas does this suggest about solving the particular marketing problem?

—How do I get beyond the intellectualizing to respondents' real feelings? I want to reach the level of unanalyzed impressions and emotions—what goes through people's minds before it becomes censored. The issue is, "What do you feel?" not "what is your opinion?" (Langer, 1978, p. 10)

The moderator must have a past-present-future time perspective throughout the discussion. Moderators must remember what has already been discussed, what is currently taking place, what the next topic of discussion will be, and, finally, what will it all mean when it is concluded.

Without doubt, the moderating process is hard work and fatiguing. Because of the mental and emotional discipline required, it is advisable not to conduct more than two focus groups on the same day.

PURPOSEFUL SMALL TALK AND PRESESSION STRATEGY

Small talk is essential just prior to beginning the group discussion and moderators must be able to talk casually and comfortably about issues of minor importance. When participants arrive for a focus group session, they are greeted by the moderator or assistant and made to feel comfortable. The participants may be asked to fill out a short registration form, which asks questions about demographic characteristics. The hosting role should be similar to that when you greet guests in your home. Emphasis is on creating a friendly, warm, and comfortable environment. Before the participants sit down, there is a period of brief, sociable small talk, and occasionally a meal is served in advance of the group interview.

The function of small talk is to create a warm and friendly environment and put the participants at ease. But, purposefully avoid the key issues to be discussed later in the session. Participants will want to express their points of view only once during the evening, and if they explain their perceptions in the informal part of the meeting, they may be reluctant to repeat the observations. Purposeful small talk avoids the focused issue and instead concentrates on common human experiences such as weather, children, or sports. Avoid controversial topics (religion, politics, or sensitive local issues) and topics that highlight differences within the group (income, education, political influence, and so on).

Because participants arrive at different times, the small talk maintains the warm and friendly environment until a sufficient number of participants are present to begin the session. In most situations, this small talk period will last only five to ten minutes, and the two-person moderating team should plan their welcoming strategy in advance. Often, one person (either moderator or assistant moderator) meets the participants at the door and brings them into the social gathering while the other person on the team visits with the group.

During this period, the moderator is observing participant interaction and noting individuals who tend to dominate the group, are excessively shy, or who consider themselves as experts. Individuals who talk a lot may later dominate the conversation and should be seated at the moderator's side if at all possible. Then, if necessary, the moderator can turn slightly away from the domineering individuals, thereby giving a nonverbal and diplomatic signal for others to talk. Shy and quiet participants are best placed immediately across from the moderator to facilitate maximum eye contact. The moderator might expect that about 40% of the participants would be eager and open to sharing insights, another 40% are more introspective and willing to talk if the situation presents itself. The remaining 20% are apprehensive about the experience and rarely share (Kelleher, 1982).

This strategic positioning of participants is achieved in the following manner. The moderating team will have a list of participants who are expected to attend the discussion and will prepare "name tents" to place on the table in front of group members. Name tents can easily be made from 5 x 8 inch cards, folded in the middle with first names printed. Last names are unnecessary. Name tents are preferred because they are larger and more legible than name tags. The moderator will casually yet carefully "drop" the name tents around the table in a seemingly random manner. In fact, the moderator has arranged the cards using observations from the informal presession, quickly checks perceptions with the assistant moderator, and then places the name tents.

Special problems often first emerge during the presession that can greatly affect the subsequent focus group interview. For example, alcohol and focus groups do not mix, either for participants or moderators. If a meal is served prior to the focus group session, be certain to inform the server that drinks will not be ordered and they should not be solicited. Participants who arrive under the influence should be quickly spotted and politely but firmly informed that their assistance will not be needed in the group interview.

Another special problem is small children. Young children running in the room or babies crying can completely upstage the discussion, at least from the moderator's perspective. Ideally, this problem is anticipated and solved in advance. When young parents are the target audience, the moderator might expect the problem and arrange for child-care services. If it happens unexpectedly, quick thinking and tactful concern on the part of the moderator can alleviate embarrassment and achieve a solution. The moderator might make a quick assessment of the child's activity level and then decide on the potential for interruptions. If the child is reasonably passive, the moderator might decide to take a risk and include the parent in the discussion. At times, the assistant moderator might function as a baby-sitter and take the child into another room. Puzzles, crayons, and coloring books could provide some temporary relief, but not for the entire 90-minute discussion.

At times, an uninvited spouse will attend the focus group session, and often there will be an extra chair to the side of the room away from the table that will be quite suitable. Some moderators will have several questionnaires in the briefcase to use with unneeded, unwanted, or overload participants. "We are asking some participants to complete this questionnaire. You may answer it in the next room, and when you are finished you may leave. Thank you for coming." Often, it is more diplomatic to request responses from overload participants using a questionnaire than to turn them away at the door.

Smoking can be a problem in focus groups. A growing number of states and institutions have established laws and guidelines that restrict smoking in meeting rooms or public locations. When focus groups are conducted with audiences familiar with and accustomed to these procedures, banning smoking is the best option. Often the easiest way to do this is by simply removing all ash trays from the room. Smoking in group environments is, at best, tolerated, and, at worst, offensive to other participants. The benefit of allowing smoking is that it may allow the smoker to satisfy a craving and relax. When conducting focus groups in environments where smokers are expected, the moderator might consider several strategies, such as

(1) holding the focus group in a well-ventilated area, perhaps even out of doors;

(2) asking participants if it would be acceptable to withhold smoking until the discussion is over;

(3) placing the smokers together at the far end of the table; or

(4) requesting smokers to slip away from the table and smoke over at the side of the room where they can hear the conversation and then rejoin the group when they are finished.

RECORDING THE GROUP DISCUSSION

Focus group sessions are typically recorded in two ways: by a tape recorder and with written notes taken by the moderator and assistant moderator. Written notes are essential. Typically, the moderator will take brief notes and the assistant will attempt to capture complete statements of the participants—especially those comments that may be quotable. The note taking should not interfere with the spontaneous nature of the group interview, and the moderator will only be able to capture brief comments by participants. If the group has to wait until the moderator finishes taking notes, the discussion will hardly be comfortable, free flowing, and relaxed.

The note taking should be done in such a manner that notes are complete and usable even if the tape recorder stops working. Tape recorders shouldn't be trusted. Murphy's Law dictates that the most insightful comment will be lost when the tape is being switched, or when background noise drowns out voices on the tape. At times, the moderator and assistant moderator may get so involved in the discussion that they both forget to monitor the tape recorder.

Tape recorders are invaluable and a must for focus group interviews. The tape-recording equipment and remote microphone are set up before the meeting begins and in plain sight of participants. Hidden recorders and microphones are usually unwise because they create an unnecessary secretive atmosphere and inhibit participant conversation if discovered. The importance of the recorder is mentioned at the beginning of the group discussion and it is introduced as a tool to help capture everyone's comments. Therefore, participants are encouraged to speak one at a time to avoid garbling the tape.

Tape-recording group conversations is difficult as recorders are prone to pick up background noise, tapping of pencils, and the hum of the ventilation system instead of the softly spoken comments of participants. Built-in microphones on cassette recorders tend to have limited sensitivity. Instead, an omni-directional remote microphone that is compatible with the tape recorder is placed with the mike in the center of the table. Recently, some moderators have had considerable success with pressure sensitive microphones, which pick up sound vibrations from the table. Occasionally, moderators use two microphones placed at different ends of the table, each connected to a recorder. Immediately before the group interview, the moderator should again test recording equipment to be sure that all comments in the room will be captured, even if spoken in quiet tones. In addition, the moderator may want to fast forward and rewind new tapes to ensure they do not stick or jam. The C-90 tapes are preferable; C-60 tapes are too short and C-120 tapes are prone to break and jam. The C-90 tape provides 90 minutes of recording time, 45 minutes per side.

BEGINNING THE
FOCUS GROUP DISCUSSION

The first few moments in focus group discussion are critical. In a brief time, the moderator must create a thoughtful, permissive atmosphere; provide the ground rules; and set the tone of the discussion. Much of the success of group interviewing can be attributed to the development of this open environment. Excessive formality and rigidity can stifle the possibility of dynamic interaction among participants. By contrast, too much informality and humor can cause problems in that participants might not take the discussion seriously. Veteran moderators testify that groups are unpredictable and one group may be exciting and free flowing while another group might be restrained, cautious, and reserved. Differences between groups are typical and should be expected; however, the moderator should introduce the group discussion in a consistent manner.

The recommended pattern for introducing the group discussion includes

(1) The welcome
(2) The overview and topic
(3) The ground rules
(4) The first question

Here is an example of a typical introduction:

Good evening and welcome to our session tonight. Thank you for taking the time to join our discussion of county educational services. My name is Dick Krueger and I represent the University of Minnesota. Assisting me is

Marsha Mueller, also from the University of Minnesota. We are attempting to gain information about educational opportunities in the community. We have invited people who live in several different parts of the county to share their perceptions and ideas.

You were randomly selected because you have certain things in common that are of particular interest to us. You are all employed outside of the home and you live in the suburban areas of the county. We are particularly interested in your views because you are representative of others in the county.

Tonight we will be discussing informal education in the community. This includes all the ways you gain new information about areas of interest to you. There are no right or wrong answers but rather differing points of view. Please feel free to share your point of view even if it differs from what others have said.

Before we begin, let me remind you of some ground rules. This is strictly a research project and there are no sales involved. Please speak up—only one person should talk at a time. We're tape-recording the session because we don't want to miss any of your comments. If several are talking at the same time, the tape will get garbled and we'll miss your comments. We will be on a first name basis tonight, and in our later reports there will not be any names attached to comments. You may be assured of complete confidentiality. Keep in mind that we're just as interested in negative comments as positive comments, and at times the negative comments are the most helpful.

Our session will last about an hour and a half, and we will not be taking a formal break. The rest rooms are just down the hall and refreshments are over near the wall. Feel free to leave the table for either of these or if you wish to stretch, but please do so quietly.

Well, let's begin. We've placed name cards on the table in front of you to help us remember each other's names. Let's find out some more about each other by going around the room one at a time. Tell us about the last time you received new information on a topic of concern. What was the topic and where did you get the information?

The first question is designed to engage all participants one at a time in the group discussion. It "breaks the ice" and gets each participant to talk. After the participant has once said something, it becomes easier to speak again. In addition, the first question underscores the common characteristics of the participants and that they all have some basis for sharing information. The responses to the first question also can serve to introduce later questions in the group interview. For example: "As we went around the room I heard you mention a variety of ways that people get information, including meetings. Would you tell us who conducted or sponsored the meetings you attended?"

In later questions, the moderator nudges the group to narrow their discussion to certain specific topics of primary concern to the study. Often, this is done by reweaving previously made comments of participants into later, more specific discussion questions. The rule of thumb is to go from general to specific, from the larger more global issues to the specific topic of concern. This deductive process helps establish a common base of communications among the participants and sets the climate for later more focused questions.

Anticipate the
Flow of the Discussion

Group discussions are unpredictable and the topics of discussion might flow precisely as planned or they might take leaps and detours. Moderators are advised to anticipate the various directions the discussion might take and be able to recognize beneficial topics of discussion as opposed to dead ends. For example, in focus groups relating to community organizations, I have found that the discussion can lead to an evaluation of agency professionals. Often, a "mock discussion" with colleagues familiar with the participants will help identify some of the varieties of responses. One of the hallmarks of a skillful moderator is flexibility in modifying the questioning route at the last minute and yet obtaining the needed information.

Give License to Expressing
Differing Points of View

Participants may need to be reminded a second time of the value of differing points of view. The introduction provides the first suggestion that all points of view—positive and negative—are needed and wanted. A second reminder is helpful if the moderator senses that participants are simply "echoing" the same concept. After several echoes on the same idea, the moderator might ask: "Does anyone see it differently?" or "Are there any other points of view?"

TWO ESSENTIAL TECHNIQUES:
THE PAUSE AND THE PROBE

Moderators of group discussions should be familiar with two essential techniques: the five-second pause and the probe. Both techniques are easy to use and helpful in soliciting additional information from group participants. The five-second pause is most often used after a participant comment. This short pause often prompts additional points of view or agreement with the previously mentioned position. There is a tendency for novice moderators to talk too much, to dominate the discussion with questions, and to move too quickly from one topic to another. Often, the short pause will elicit additional points of view, especially when coupled with eye contact from the moderator. The five-second pause can be practiced on family, friends, and coworkers with interesting results. Advance practice allows the moderator to become familiar with this technique, so it can be used comfortably in group interviews.

The second essential technique is the probe, the request for additional information. In most conversations and group discussions, there is a tendency for people to make vague comments that could have multiple meanings or to say "I agree." When this occurs, the probe is an effective technique to elicit additional information. Typically, probing involves such comments as

"Would you explain further?"

"Would you give me an example of what you mean?"

"Would you say more?"

"Is there anything else?"

"Please describe what you mean"

"I don't understand."

It is usually best to use the probe early in the interview to communicate the importance of precision in responses and then use it sparingly in later discussion. For example, if a participant indicates agreement by saying "I agree" then the moderator should follow up with: "Tell us more," or "What experiences have you had that make you feel that way?" A few probes used in this way underscore the impression that more detailed answers are needed and wanted. Excessive probing, however, can be extremely time consuming and unnecessary.

RESPONDING TO PARTICIPANT COMMENTS

Moderators should be attentive to how they respond to comments from participants—both verbal and nonverbal. Often, these moderator responses are unconscious habits from past social interactions. Self-discipline and practice are needed to overcome habits such as the following:

(1) Head nodding. Some moderators will continually nod their heads as comments are being made. Head nodding at times can be helpful if used sparingly and consciously such as in eliciting additional comments from participants. Unfortunately, it is often an unconscious response that signals agreement and, as a result, tends to elicit additional comments of the same type. Similarly, the negative nod with the head going side to side tends to signal to the participant that the comment is not needed, not wanted, or wrong. As a rule of thumb, beginning moderators should try to restrict their head nodding tendencies.

(2) Short verbal responses. In many of our typical social interactions, we have become conditioned to providing short verbal responses that signal approval or acceptance. Many of these are acceptable within the focus group environment, such as *OK, yes,* or *uh huh,* but others should be avoided if they communicate indications of accuracy or agreement. Responses to avoid include *correct, that's good,* or *excellent* because they imply judgments about the quality of the comment.

Aspiring moderators should be encouraged to practice these techniques within their normal social interactions and become comfortable with "value neutral" gestures and comments. Practice focus group sessions and coaching advice from others can also prove helpful.

THE EXPERT, THE DOMINANT TALKER, THE SHY PARTICIPANT, AND THE RAMBLER

One of the exciting aspects of focus group discussions is that it brings together a variety of people with differing backgrounds and characteristics. Sometimes, however, individual characteristics can present special problems for the moderator. These four types of participants—the expert, the dominant talker, the shy participant, and the rambler—regularly participate in focus groups, and each type presents special problems.

Self-appointed "experts" can present special problems in focus groups. What they say and how they say it can have an inhibiting influence on others in the group. Participants often defer to others who are perceived to have more education, affluence, or political/social influence. Some people consider themselves experts because they have had considerable experience with the topic under discussion, because they hold positions of influence in the community, or because they have previously participated in this type of session. Often, the best way of handling experts is to underscore the fact that everyone is an expert and all participants have important perceptions that need to be expressed. In addition, the introductory question should avoid responses that would identify participants' levels of education, affluence, or social/political influence.

Dominant talkers sometimes consider themselves to be experts, but much of the time they are unaware of how they are perceived by others. Often dominant talkers are spotted in presession small talk. As indicated earlier in this chapter, attempt to seat the dominant individual beside the moderator in order to exercise control by the use of body language. When this strategy does not work, then the more frontal tactic of verbally shifting attention is required. For example: "Thank you, John. Are there others who wish to comment on the question?" or "Does anyone feel differently?" or "That's one point of view. Does anyone have another point of view?" Other nonverbal techniques also can be used such as avoiding eye contact with the talker and appearing bored with the comments. Most important, be tactful and kind because harsh and critical comments may curtail spontaneity from others in the group.

Shy respondents tend to say little and speak with soft voices. Garrison Keillor has suggested that Powdermilk Biscuits give shy people the strength to do what needs to be done. Unfortunately, these biscuits are not readily available—if they were, the experts would probably eat them all anyway—so other measures are needed to encourage shy respondents. Extra effort is required to get these individuals to elaborate their views and to feel that their comments are wanted and appreciated. If possible, the moderator should place shy respondents directly across the table to maximize eye contact. Eye contact often provides sufficient encouragement to speak, and, if all else fails, the moderator can call on them by name.

Rambling respondents use a lot of words and usually never get to the point, if they have a point. These individuals are comfortable with talking and seem to feel an obligation to say something. Unfortunately, the rambling respondent can drone on and on and eat up precious discussion time. As a rule of thumb, I usually discontinue eye contact with the rambler after about 20-30 seconds. The assistant moderator should do likewise. Look at your papers, look at the other participants, turn your body away from the speaker, look bored, look at your watch, but don't look at the rambler. As soon as the rambler stops or pauses, the moderator should be ready to fire away with the next question or repeat the current question being discussed. In the remainder of the discussion, the moderating team should limit eye contact with the rambling participant.

SELECTING THE
FOCUS GROUP LOCATION

Focus group interviews have been successfully conducted in a variety of locations such as restaurants, hotel rooms, private homes, public buildings, and so on. A primary consideration is that the location is easy to find. Private homes may be difficult for other participants to locate, but they do offer a relaxed informal environment. Private homes are acceptable if they are easy for participants to locate and if directions are clearly provided in the letter of invitation. The room should be free from outside distractions. Meeting places that have visual or audio distractions should be avoided. If at all possible, the moderator should "scout out" the location in advance and watch for factors that could interrupt or interfere with the group session. For example, tape recording is nearly impossible in some locations due to background music or the hum of ventilation systems. Attempt to eliminate visual distractions to the participants. Some rooms have large windows and are close to open doors and hallways where the traffic flow causes constant interruption. A large screen television set that can be seen from the discussion room can also distract participants.

The environment for the focus group should be neutral. At times, the location of the session will influence the type of responses provided by participants. Effort is sometimes made initially to conceal the identity of those sponsoring the group interview to avoid advance bias and participant self-selection. Therefore, a meeting room in the sponsoring organization is probably not a wise environment. Nonprofit organizations, perhaps more than private businesses, seem to have an image that can influence how people respond in that environment. Library meeting rooms, police conference rooms, courthouse meeting rooms, church basements have potential to evoke inhibitions or reactions among participants.

The room should have chairs that can be arranged with participants facing each other. Tables are often desirable because they enable participants to lean forward and be less self-conscious about their bodies. Eye contact among all participants is vital, and having participants equally spaced around a table is strongly preferable.

Market research firms regularly use specially designed rooms with oval tables, built in microphones, and a one-way mirror behind the moderator. Behind the mirror is a special viewing room for clients where they can observe and listen to the proceedings. Market research firms differ in terms of how much attention they place on the one-way mirror. In some situations, it is pointed out to the participants and described as a way for the clients to hear consumer comments. In other situations, the mirror is not mentioned, and, at times, the mirror is constructed to appear unobtrusive. In some circumstances, the session is also video-taped from behind the one-way mirror.

I have shied away from these room arrangements because of limited availability in many communities as well as the secretive image of one-way mirrors. I have avoided videotaping the groups, but for a different reason. Videotaping is obtrusive and simply not worth the effort. I have found that it invariably changes the environment and affects the participant spontaneity. Videotaping usually requires several cameras plus camera operators who attempt to swing cameras quickly to follow the flowing conversation. The fuss and fury of videotaping makes the focus group appear more like a circus than a discussion.

BE READY FOR THE UNEXPECTED

One should prepare for the unexpected by thinking about the possible things that can go wrong. Here are some of the things that might go wrong, and possible courses of action:

(1) Nobody shows up. Review your letter of invitation to be certain you are at the right location on the correct date. Telephone a few of the participants to see if they are coming and if they have received the invitation. Always take a list of invited participants with their phone numbers to the discussion location.

(2) Only a few attend. Conduct the session anyway, but after the meeting check to be certain that all people received the written letter of invitation and telephone reminder.

(3) The meeting place is inadequate. Improvise, but attempt to spot this in advance. Arrive at the interview location well in advance of the participants, especially if it is a location that you have not used before.

(4) The group doesn't want to talk. Consider calling on individuals, or going around the group answering a specific question. Use pauses and probes. Consider revising the questions to add more interest.

(5) The group gets so involved that they don't want to leave. A delightful problem that does occasionally occur. Stay awhile and listen

to the conversation if your time permits. Formally adjourn the meeting, pack up, and leave.

(6) Hazardous weather occurs just hours before the meeting. Phone each person to let them know the session has been canceled.

(7) The early questions take too much time, leaving little time to ask the final questions. Pace the questions and monitor the clock during the interview to allow enough time for the final questions. Often, the last questions are the most focused and revealing. Before the interview, pretend that you've only asked half of the questions and five minutes remain. Consider how you would ask the remaining questions.

CONCLUDING THE FOCUS GROUP

The moderator has several options for closing the focus group. Perhaps the most common procedure is simply to thank the group for participating, provide them with the gift or cash if promised, and wish them a safe journey home. An alternative is for the moderator to summarize briefly the main points of view and ask if this perception is accurate. This task of summarization is often helpful to the moderator in the subsequent analysis process. It is the first opportunity the moderator has to pull together the overall group discussion. When presenting the brief summary, the moderator should watch the body language of the participants for signs of agreement, hesitation, or confusion. If the group does not seem to agree with the summary of the comments, the moderator should ask for clarification. Still another tactic for closure is describing the purpose of the study and asking an open-ended question of the participants. "Do you have any additional thoughts?" or "Is there anything missing from our conversation?" Both work very nicely. A variation of this strategy is useful if participants are reluctant to talk because of sensitivity to the recording equipment. The variation is to turn off the recording equipment, indicate that the discussion is now completed, thank them for their assistance, and then ask "Do you think we've missed anything in the discussion?" This closure may uncover some avenues of thought that were not anticipated.

SUMMARY

There is a lot to think about in preparing to moderate a focus group interview. The logistics and equipment should be checked out in advance and then crossed off a worry list. The most frequent danger of novice moderators is that they worry about too many things just before the group session and consequently begin the discussion with high anxiety. The best advice for beginning moderators is to practice asking questions, worry several days before the focus group, and then relax just before the discussion.

A characteristic of focus group interviews is that participants will often compensate for the awkward questions of the moderator and provide enlightening answers. It's hard to predict in advance how a focus group session will go. Groups vary greatly and flexibility is essential. Ask the unexpected questions that emerge from the discussion, but avoid major detours in the questioning route. Consider the various strategies for bringing closure to the discussion. Throughout the discussion, the moderating team should remember that they are visitors in the world of the participants and, for a brief time, they are sharing the reality of the participants' environment. The permissive moderator allows the discussion to flow, and topics may be introduced in a different sequence from what was originally anticipated.

APPENDIX:
CHECKLIST FOR FOCUS GROUP INTERVIEWS

Advance Notice

___ Contact participants by phone one to two weeks before the session.
___ Send each participant a letter of invitation.
___ Give the participants a reminder phone call prior to the session.
___ Slightly overrecruit the number of participants.

Questions

___ The introductory question should be answered quickly and not identify status.
___ Questions should flow in a logical sequence.
___ Key questions should focus on the critical issues of concern.
___ Use considered probe or follow-up questions.
___ Limit the use of "why" questions.
___ Use "think back" questions as needed.

Logistics

___ The room should be satisfactory (size, tables, comfort, and so on).
___ The moderator arrives early to make necessary changes.
___ Background noise should not interfere with the tape-recording.
___ Have name tags and/or name tents for participants.
___ A remote microphone should be placed on the table.
___ Bring extra tapes, batteries, and extension cords.
___ Plan topics for small talk conversation.
___ Seat experts and loud participants next to the moderator.
___ Seat shy and quiet participants directly across from moderator.

___ When having a meal, limit selections and stress fast service.
___ Bring enough copies of handouts and/or visual aids.

Moderator Skills

___ Be well rested and alert for the focus group session.
___ Practice introduction without referring to notes.
___ Remember questions without referring to notes.
___ Be cautious to avoid head nodding.
___ Avoid comments that signal approval, that is, "excellent," "great," "wonderful."
___ Avoid giving personal opinions.

Immediately After the Session

___ Prepare a brief written summary of key points as soon as possible.
___ Check to see if the tape recorder captured the comments.

6

Participants in a Focus Group

People are essential for a focus group! Of all the elements of focus group interviewing, the most overlooked and underestimated aspect is recruitment of the right people. Careful preparation, trained moderators, and quality questions are important, but these are of limited value if the right people don't attend. Too often, public sector organizations and institutions underestimate the importance of careful recruitment of participants. Who should be invited? How many people should participate? How should participants be identified? What can be done to ensure that participants actually attend? How many groups should be conducted? Public institutions, and especially nonprofit organizations, often have difficulty because they assume that getting volunteers is one of their strengths. After all, people come to meetings now, so can't they use their traditional means of soliciting and advertising for focus group participants? The answer is NO! The old methods may be suitable for meetings, events, or activities, but they lack the deliberate features that ensure that exactly the correct number of the right people will attend.

The first ingredient in successful recruitment is to realize that special efforts must be made, especially in nonprofit organizations. In working with focus groups, most nonprofits might as well forget about their traditional means for recruitment and substitute a systematic and deliberate process. Conventional methods such as newsletters, form letter invitations, or announcements at meetings yield disappointing results. If the organization is truly interested in getting quality information, then these older methods should be set aside, because they will not be effective in getting the correct number of the right people to attend.

THE PURPOSE DRIVES THE STUDY

To decide who should be invited to the group interview, think about the purpose of the study. Usually the purpose is to make statements about people—specifically about people who have certain things in common. This purpose should now guide the invitation decisions. The statement of purpose may require some additional refinement and clarification to ensure the audience is precisely defined. It is vital to identify the target group as precisely as possible, and this then becomes the unit of analysis. For example, the researcher might have initially identified community residents, but later, after some thought, restricted the audience to unmarried residents between the ages of 18 and 40. In other situations, the key unit of analysis might be stated in broad terms such as homemakers, teenagers, or residents of a geographic area.

The purpose of the study dictates the degree of specification needed in the target audience. If an organization is interested in reaching new members and wants to use focus groups to discover those features that would prompt attendance, then a decision is needed. What type of members is it seeking to attract—teenagers, young families, single-parent families, seniors, and so on? If several different audiences are sought, then it is advisable to conduct a series of focus groups with each audience category. It may be impossible to determine in advance the extent to which groups differ in terms of organizational attendance, but it would seem reasonable that age and family characteristics would be a logical starting point.

THE COMPOSITION OF THE GROUP

The focus group is characterized by homogeneity, but with sufficient variation among participants to allow for contrasting opinions. Most commonly, homogeneity is sought in terms of occupation, social class, educational level, age, education, or family characteristics. The guiding principle is the degree to which these factors will influence sharing within the group discussion. Some mixes of participants do not work well because of limited understanding of other life-styles and situations. For example, care must be exercised in mixing individuals from different life stages and styles—young working women with home-makers in their fifties who have not been employed outside of the home—unless the topic clearly cuts across these life stages and styles. Often, participants will be inhibited and defer to those whom they perceive to be more experienced, knowledgeable, or better educated. A small degree of variation within group characteristics is often a helpful way to obtain the contrast and variation that spark lively discussions. Unfortunately, it doesn't work well to divide the group up into thirds with equal numbers from three contrasting groups and expect the discussion to be a forum of differing points of view. A more workable strategy is either to conduct a separate series of focus groups with each segment or to target the most important group if resources are limited.

At times, it is unwise to mix sexes in focus groups, particularly if the topic of discussion is experienced differently by each sex. Men may have a tendency to speak more frequently and with more authority when in groups with women—sometimes called the "peacock effect"—and consequently this can be an irritant to the women in the group. Myril Axelrod (1975a, p. 5) recommends against mixing sexes in a focus group because "men tend to 'perform' for the women and vice versa."

A related topic is the involvement of both husband and wife in the same focus group discussion. I have found that there is a tendency for one spouse to remain silent and defer to the talkative spouse. Even if the silent spouse disagrees, it appears that he or she is reluctant to comment even when such comments are solicited from the moderator. As a result, I have found that focus groups of four married couples turn out to be discussions with only four people.

THE SIZE OF A FOCUS GROUP

Traditionally, the ideal focus group is composed of seven to ten people with similar backgrounds. Focus groups with more than twelve participants are not recommended: they limit each person's opportunity to share insights and observations. In addition, group dynamics change when participants are not able to describe their experiences. For example, if people do not have an opportunity to share experiences in the total group, they may lean over to the next person to whisper observations. This phenomenon is clearly a signal that the group is too large. Small focus groups, or mini-focus groups, with four to six participants are becoming increasingly popular because the smaller groups are easier to recruit, host, and more comfortable for participants. The disadvantage of the mini-focus group is that it limits the total range of experiences simply because the group is smaller. Four people will have had fewer total experiences than a dozen.

Often, the nature of the questioning route and participant characteristics yield clues as to the ideal size. Focus groups with specialized audiences where the intent is to get more in-depth insights are usually accomplished best by smaller groups. Also, smaller groups are preferable when the participants have a great deal to share about the topic or have had intense or lengthy experiences with the topic of discussion. In other discussions where the researcher wants to discover the range of perceptions in more general terms, larger groups are preferable.

IDENTIFYING THE PARTICIPANTS

The process of identification and recruitment of focus group participants is considerably easier when begun with names, addresses, and phone numbers of participants who meet the criteria for inclusion. In these cases, existing directories, membership lists, or organizational records can be consulted to identify potential candidates. Screening processes are needed when membership lists or organizational records are unavailable. Several strategies are available for locating participants for a focus group interview. The most commonly used procedures include using existing lists, contacting existing groups, seeking referrals from current participants, and random telephone screening. A less common procedure, but useful for some nonprofit organizations, is to recruit on location, such as at a park, a fair, or a community event.

(1) Usually the preferred choice is an existing list. One of the most convenient ways of finding participants is to use existing lists of people. This could include existing lists of clients, members, or those who use services of the organization. Some of these preexisting lists are well maintained and revised regularly to reflect address changes, but other times the lists contain substantial errors. Typically, lists provide more names than are needed and either a systematic or random sampling procedure should be used in picking the actual names. In a systematic sample, each "n-th" number is picked to be in the selection pool. For example, if ten names are needed from a list of 200, every 20th person on the list is selected. The random sample consists of drawing names or ID numbers out of the hat, or using a random number table to select from the list of 200 people.

(2) An alternative strategy is to contact other groups for names. Once the audience has been targeted and the necessary characteristics for individual selection have been determined, the researcher might investigate whether existing groups in the community have members with these characteristics. Some groups will be reluctant to release names or will have formal restrictions on releasing member lists. Cooperation is more

likely if the researcher explains that there is no selling, that volunteers can decline to participate, and that participants will receive a gift. In some situations, a contribution to the group treasury, tactfully offered, can be a reflection of the value placed on assistance in obtaining names of volunteers.

(3) Participants in focus groups can be asked for names. Participants in focus groups can often suggest names of others who meet the necessary characteristics. This approach works only when there is adequate time delay between focus groups and when the rewards of participation are obvious and preferably monetary. It is more comfortable for people to suggest names of friends and neighbors when participation results in a cash gift.

Another variation of this procedure is the "snowball sampling" procedure. With this snowball approach, the invited participant is requested to bring a friend to the discussion.

(4) Use random telephone screening. A fourth method of obtaining focus group participants is by telephone screening. The procedure typically begins by random selection of names from a telephone directory. A series of screening questions are used to determine if those called meet the criteria established for the focus group. This method is a favorite of many market research firms because they are able to control the quantity of calls and consequently the number who will be attending the group interview. Two sample screening questionnaires are included in the appendixes.

Telephone screening is most efficient when searching for participants with fairly common characteristics. As the number of screens increases, the efficiency of this procedure will decrease. For example, in an effort to reach working homemakers, it was necessary to call 50 households in order to identify 25 working homemakers. Only 10 of these were able and willing to participate in a focus group interview at the designated time. If the screen had been more restrictive—for example, working homemakers with children between the ages of 5 to 10—then the efficiency of the calling procedure would decrease.

The efficiency of the telephone screening procedures is also affected by the skills of the interviewer. Friendly and sincere calls that convey interest and enthusiasm are most effective. Several years ago, I had an opportunity to work cooperatively with a market research company in helping a community nonprofit organization. The nonprofit organization had employed several college students and used a predetermined interviewing script for calling. The students were finding that people did pass through the screens but then often declined the invitation to attend the discussion. The percentage of invitations accepted dramatically increased when a professional moderator began making the phone calls. The professional conveyed a sense of confidence, friendliness, and sincerity that was developed after years of experience. Because invitations over the phone are often regarded with suspicion, those making the invitations require considerable communication skill.

(5) Some nonprofit organizations are able to recruit "on location" by inviting people using the services to participate in a discussion. For example, a nature center, zoo, or recreational center might intercept a random assortment of people passing through the gate and invite them to a special discussion. The incentive for participation might be free tickets for another visit.

SAMPLING PROCEDURES FOR
FOCUS GROUPS

When researchers approach focus group interviewing, they carry with them many of the traditions, wisdom, and procedures that were intended for experimental and quantifiable studies. Some of these procedures readily transfer, but others do not. The issue of sampling procedures requires some special thought when planning focus group interviews.

Most researchers have "cut their teeth" on randomization and, because these procedures have served them well in some arenas, they may assume that the same procedures are also appropriate for qualitative studies in general and focus group interviews in particular. Randomization essentially removes the bias in selection—that is, all participants possess an equivalent chance to be involved in the study. Random selection is particularly appropriate when inferences are made to a larger population because of the assumption that opinions, attitudes, or whatever being studied will be normally distributed within that population. Therefore, a random sample of sufficient size will be an adequate substitute for surveying the entire population.

It is important to keep in mind that the intent of focus groups is not to infer but to understand, not to generalize but to determine the range, and not to make statements about the population but to provide insights about how people perceive a situation. As a result, focus groups require a flexible research design, and while a degree of randomization may be used, it is not the primary factor in selection.

The driving force in participant selection is the purpose of the study. Once again, researchers must focus on why the study is being conducted and about whom statements will be made. While the purpose dictates the nature of the selection, the process is also tempered by practical concerns and the credibility of the study. With all sampling strategies, the researcher must be concerned about the degree to which that strategy could lead to distortions in the data. The researcher should anticipate questions about the means of selection and provide the rationale for those decisions.

THE DANGER OF EXISTING GROUPS

At times, the focus group interview is used with groups that are already established such as employee work groups, boards of directors, or professional colleagues. These existing groups may have formal or informal ways of relating to each other that can influence their responses. Superior-subordinate relationships among participants can inhibit discussion. The focus group technique works well when all participants are on an equal basis. If supervisors, bosses, or even a friend of the boss are in the group, the results might be affected. In addition, there might be a reluctance to express negative observations in front of coworkers, especially if supervisors are present. Focus group should be conducted without the presence of supervisors, and, if necessary, a special group session can be conducted for supervisors. It is critical to assure confidentiality to all participants and to remind them that their names will not be attached to the final report.

NUMBER OF GROUPS NEEDED

When compared to quantitative survey methods, the number of different individuals and groups involved in a focus group study is surprisingly small. A helpful rule of thumb is to continue conducting interviews until little new information is provided. Typically, the first two groups provide a considerable amount of new information, but by the third or fourth session, a fair amount may have already been covered. If this occurs, there is limited value in continuing with additional group discussions with that particular audience segment. So the suggested rule of thumb is to plan for four groups with similar audiences, but evaluate after the third group. If new insights are provided in the third group, then conduct the fourth and additional groups as needed.

The recommendation of four focus groups is conditioned by the nature of the study, the diversity of the participants' exposure to the topic of discussion, and differences that reflect social, ethnic, or geographic diversity. In some situations, it is highly advisable to go beyond four focus groups. More groups are advisable when participants are heterogeneous, or when statewide or national-level insights are wanted.

Fewer groups will be needed if the study is intended to provide helpful insights about an easily reversible program decision. For example, occasionally, focus groups are conducted to determine how a new program will be received. If the new program involves a slight realignment of staff time and does not require an additional investment for staff or buildings, fewer groups are probably appropriate. If, however, focus groups are intended to assist decision makers in making major decisions that were hard to reverse (new buildings, hiring more staff, and so on), then more focus groups would be warranted.

The topic of the focus group interview might relate to a narrow category of people with similar backgrounds who have had the same level of exposure to the program. Consequently, fewer focus groups would be needed. In other circumstances, the people may be exposed to differing levels of the program, and each category of participant may have different perceptions. This diversity of exposure to the issue of investigation would favor increasing the number of focus groups.

GETTING PEOPLE TO
ATTEND THE FOCUS GROUP

A number of years ago, my colleagues and I began conducting focus groups for nonprofit organizations. Some of these early experiences with focus groups were disastrous because so few people showed up for the discussion. Invitations were extended in the same way that we had traditionally invited people to other types of meetings, seminars, or workshops. As we analyzed what had gone wrong, we discovered several major flaws in our traditional invitations. Our invitations were not personalized, we had no follow-up to the original written invitation, we were requesting people to take time to attend a discussion on a seemingly insignificant topic, we were unaware of the seasonal time demands on some audiences, we did not build on existing social and organizational relationships, and, finally, we did not offer incentives.

Invitations to focus groups should be personalized. Each participant should feel that they are personally needed and wanted at the interview. Staff members who make telephone invitations should receive special training and practice to extend warm and sincere requests for participants—without sounding like the invitation is being read. The invitation should stress that the potential participant has special experiences or insights that would be of value in the study. Form letters prepared on a mimeograph or copy machine are not personal. They should be replaced by individual letters on letterhead stationary that are signed by the moderator.

Systematic notification procedures provide the necessary follow-up on invitations. This involves a series of sequential activities, including the following:

(1) Establishing meeting times for the group interviews that don't conflict with existing community activities or functions. Some people have time schedules that change on a regular and predictable basis. Farmers, tax consultants, certain small businessmen in rural communities, and teachers are but a few examples. Focus groups are best conducted during their slack or off season. For example, I have avoided conducting focus groups with Minnesota farmers from mid-April to early August, and again from early September to late October. On a related note, care should be taken to avoid dates that conflict with popular sporting events (local or college teams, the World Series, Monday Night Football, and so on), national events (political conventions, elections, and so on), or periods of high television viewing (rating weeks, beginning of fall network shows, and so on).

(2) Contacting potential participants via phone approximately 10-14 days before the meeting. When using a random telephone screening procedure, an immediate invitation is extended to those passing through the screening questions. Usually it is best to overrecruit at this initial stage, perhaps by as much as 25%.

(3) Sending a personalized invitation one week before the session. The letter is sent on official letterhead with a personal salutation, an inside address, and containing the signature of the sender. It provides additional details about the session, location, and topic of discussion. An example of the letter is included in the appendixes.

(4) Phoning each person the day before the focus group reminding them of the session and inquiring about their intention to attend.

People are more likely to take time to attend a focus group interview if they believe the study is of importance. The sense of importance is conveyed in several ways, one of which is in providing gifts or cash to participants. Importance is also conveyed by holding the interviews in a prestigious location or by serving refreshments. The least expensive way to convey importance is by describing the social value of the study or the usefulness of the study to decision makers or to community residents. The researcher is thereby presented as the link between the respondent and those who will be making decisions on the future of the program.

Incentives to participate should be considered. This might include a free meal, a gift, or cash. Gifts include such items as telephones, alarm clocks, calculators, and so on, which can often be purchased for $5 to $20. These gifts tend to be a symbol that the researcher is giving something in exchange for what has been received. The use of a gift helps promote goodwill between the participants and the sponsoring agency. In some situations, a cash incentive is most effective and will range from $10 to over $100 for participants who are particularly difficult to recruit. Market research firms tend to use a three-tier scale for financial incentives.

Level 1—$15-$25: Participants who are relatively easy to locate within a community; for example, female/male head of household.

Level 2—$25-$50: Participants who must meet a number of criteria, are harder to reach than those in Level 1, or who can be expected to have conflicts in their schedules; for example: middle management or engineers.

Level 3—$75-$100 +: Participants who must meet precise criteria, are underrepresented in the community, are on very busy schedules, or who expect significant compensation; for example, physicians or top management.

A positive, upbeat invitation; the opportunity to share opinions, meals, or refreshments; and tangible gifts are all helpful incentives for potential participants. So is a convenient and easy to find meeting location. It is also helpful if they know they will be participating in an important research project where their opinions will be of particular value. A number of people have a natural curiosity and an interest in sharing their opinions. They feel honored when they are asked to provide opinions for a research project. Finally, people are more likely to attend a focus group if the invitation builds on some existing community, social, or personal relationship. Thus an invitation might mention the connection between the study and a local organization.

IDENTIFICATION OF THE SPONSOR

Who's sponsoring the study? This is one of the first questions asked by some people when they receive a telephone invitation to participate in a group discussion. When a market research firm offers invitations to a focus group interview, they will use their agency name and letterhead but will not reveal the specific client or product being tested. They will describe it as a type or category of product, such as soft drinks, farm pesticides, or automobiles. Care is taken to avoid naming the specific product so that participants will not come with presuppositions. Excessive background information encourages participants to offer solutions to the client's problem as opposed to the intended purpose—that of identifying the nature of the problem. Also, too much advance information may prompt some participants to "research" the topic, discuss it with others in advance, or rehearse their opinions. These activities have a tendency to cause respondents to act like experts and trap them into a point of view that they feel they need to defend. Furthermore, knowing the name of the product might bias comments in the group discussion. It is often best to anticipate that people will inquire about who is sponsoring the study, and to have a generic response that provides an answer without influencing later responses. At the end of the focus group session, the participants can be provided more specific information on the sponsorship and purpose of the study.

Nonprofit organizations conducting their own focus groups should give special thought to how they will respond to questions about the sponsorship of the study. Premature revelation of the sponsor can bias later responses, and yet the answer must be truthful. Truthful responses need not be all inclusive, and it may be sufficient to describe the sponsor as a subunit of the organization or a higher level in the same organization. For example, community education might be described as a study sponsored by the school district. A human services department may be identified as county or state government.

SUMMARY

Focus groups require participants, and, to be effective, they must be the right participants. Homogeneity is the guiding principle for focus groups, and the researcher much determine the nature of that homogeneity based on the purpose of the study. Participants can be recruited in a variety of ways including lists or directories, through cooperating organizations or individuals, by telephone screening, or "on location" at an event or activity. Care should be exercised when conducting focused interviews with existing groups or organizations.

People often ask how many focus group sessions should be conducted. There is no universal answer, but the helpful rule of thumb is initially to plan four sessions and then modify the number as needed. If nothing new emerges after the third session, then the fourth can be canceled. If new insights and opinions continue to develop at the fourth session, then more should be added. When the same themes repeat, it is time to stop interviewing and write the report. Incentives and systematic invitation procedures help guarantee attendance. People are often skeptical about attending meetings where the purpose or sponsor is unknown. Respect the cautious attitude of potential participants by providing sincere, sensitive, and upbeat encouragement.

APPENDIX A

TELEPHONE SCREENING QUESTIONNAIRE
Farmers of 160 to 440 acres

Name _____ Date_____

Address_____ Phone ( )_____

Hello, my name is _____ and I'm calling from the University of Minnesota in St. Paul. We are conducting a short survey of heads of households. Would that be you?

[IF YES, CONTINUE. IF NO, ASK FOR HEAD OF HOUSEHOLD]

We are conducting a farming survey that will take less than 2 minutes. Is it OK to begin?

1 Would you say that most of your income is from farming or from non-farm sources?
    ( ) Farming   [CONTINUE]
    ( ) Non-Farm   [TERMINATE]

2. How many acres do you farm?
    ( )   less than 160 acres. [TERMINATE]
    ( )   160-220 acres   [RECRUIT AT LEAST 6]
    ( )   221-320 acres   [RECRUIT AT LEAST 6]
    ( )   321-440 acres   [RECRUIT AT LEAST 6]
    ( )   over 441 acres   [TERMINATE]

3. [BY OBSERVATION, RESPONDENT IS]:
    ( )   Male
    ( )   Female

We are asking selected people to join us for a discussion about continuing education programs in agriculture. The discussion will be at the _____ on _____ at _____ and will last about one and one-half hours. Coffee and rolls will be served. Would you be able to join us at that time?

( )   Yes, Name: _____
( )   No [IF NO] Thank you for answering our questions.

[IF YES] I will be sending you a letter confirming this information. Should I use the address of _____? [CONFIRM ADDRESS] If you need any help with directions or if you need to cancel, please call our office at _____. Thank you very much for your cooperation.

APPENDIX B

TELEPHONE SCREENING QUESTIONNAIRE
Working Women Between 25 and 49 in Fairview County

Interviewee Name _____ Date _____

Address _____ Phone ( ) _____

Hello, my name is _____, and I'm calling for Northern Research in Minneapolis. We are conducting a short survey in Fairview County and I would like to talk to a woman in the household who works outside of the home. Is that person available?

[IF AVAILABLE THEN CONTINUE. IF NOT, THEN TERMINATE]
Northern Research is conducting a study on informal education in Fairview County and I would like to ask you a few questions. The questions will take less than 2 minutes. Is it OK to begin?

1. Do you live in Fairview County?
   ( ) Yes   [CONTINUE]
   ( ) No   [TERMINATE]

2. Are you employed full time or part time outside the home?
   ( ) Full time   [CONTINUE]
   ( ) Part time   [TERMINATE]

3. In what age category do you belong?
   ( ) Under 25   [TERMINATE]
   ( ) 25-34   [RECRUIT AT LEAST 8]
   ( ) 35-49   [RECRUIT AT LEAST 8]
   ( ) 50 or over [TERMINATE]

[PARTICIPANT RECRUITMENT]
Ms. _____, Northern Research is sponsoring a meeting with working women in Fairview County to discuss informal education. We know that working women are busy and yet they get new information and education from a variety of sources. We would like you to join a group of other working women as we discuss this topic. This is not a sales meeting, but strictly a research project. It will be held on Thursday evening, December 3rd at the Riverside Restaurant in Conover. We would like you to be our guest for dinner which will begin at 7:00 p.m. The meeting will be over at 9:30 p.m. Will you be able to attend?

   ( ) Yes   [CONFIRM NAME AND ADDRESS]
   ( ) No   [THANK AND TERMINATE]

[IF YES] I will be sending you a letter in a few days confirming this meeting. If you need any help with directions or if you need to cancel, please call our office at _____. Thank you and goodbye.

APPENDIX C
Sample Letter of Invitation to Focus Group
OFFICIAL LETTERHEAD

[Date]

[Name and address
of participant]

Thank you for accepting our invitation to attend the discussion at the Riverside Restaurant in Conover on Thursday, December 3rd. The Riverside Restaurant is on Highway 42 on the north side of town. We would like you to be our guest for dinner which will begin at 7:00 p.m. The meeting will follow the meal and conclude by 9:30 p.m.

Since we are talking to a limited number of people, the success and quality of our discussion is based on the cooperation of the people who attend. Because you have accepted our invitation, your attendance at the session is anticipated and will aid in making the research project a success.

The discussion you will be attending will be a forum of women in the community who are employed outside of the home. We will be discussing information sources and educational opportunities and we would like to get your opinions on this subject. This is strictly a research project, and no sales or solicitations will be made. At the conclusion of the session we will be giving you a small token of our appreciation.

If for some reason you find you are not able to attend, please call us to let us know as soon as possible. Our phone number is (612) 624-2221.

We look forward to seeing you on December 3.

Sincerely,

Dick Krueger
Forum Moderator

7

Analyzing Focus Group Results

A statement of what data analysis is—

Data analysis consists of examining, categorizing, tabulating, or otherwise recombining the evidence, to address the initial propositions of a study. (Yin, 1984, p. 99)

A story of what data analysis is not—

Once upon a time an institution of higher learning set out to hire a new president. The governing board of the institution sought applications from far and near but because of the limited travel budget only the near applications were seriously considered. It turned out that three professors were among the final candidates to be interviewed by the board. The first was a professor of accounting, the second was a professor of engineering, and the third was a professor who regularly served as a management consultant. After completing all interviews the board was deadlocked. In an attempt to resolve the dilemma the board decided to invite all three professors back to answer one final question. The accounting professor was the first to be asked: "What is two plus two?" The professor immediately replied, "With great confidence I can tell you that the answer is exactly four." The engineering professor was the second candidate to be asked the question: "What is two plus two?" After a moment of reflection the engineer replied: "In the field of engineering we are accustomed to problems such as this. In engineering we frequently must deal with numbers that are rounded. Therefore the first two could be any number between 1.50 and 2.49 and the same is true of the second number. This means that the sum of two plus two could be any number between 3.00 and 4.98. Finally the board invited the management consultant into the board room. The question was asked: "What is two plus two?" The consultant slowly got up from the chair and went over to shut the door, then over to the window to close the blinds, and finally back to the board table. The consultant leaned across the table and with a low voice, slightly over a whisper, he asked: "What do you want it to be?"

Qualitative analysis is not whatever you want it to be, but unfortunately that is a perception that is sometimes held. The intent of this chapter is to present an overview of focus group analysis that is practical, systematic, and verifiable.

Analysis can be a stumbling block for qualitative researchers. The unanticipated volume of data is sobering, but more often it is the complexity of the analysis that stops the researcher cold. In some situations, researchers have been accused of overlooking important evidence, ignoring critical factors, or twisting facts to meet earlier assumptions.

THE BEGINNING OF ANALYSIS

Analysis begins by going back to the intent of the study. Indeed, throughout the analysis process, the researcher should remember the purpose of the study. Qualitative researchers have been known to be overwhelmed with the vast accumulation of data and find that they have a multitude of choices. A key principle is to remember the purpose of the study and to use the depth or intensity of analysis appropriate to the problem. At times, the purpose of the study is narrow, and elaborate analysis is unneeded and inappropriate. For example, suppose that focus groups are to provide insights and appropriate vocabulary to use in a mail-out survey. Contrast this to a more complex situation where the researcher wants to understand the processes that potential clientele use in deciding whether or not to participate in a new educational opportunity.

The beginning principle of analysis is that the problem drives the analysis. Difficulties emerge in both qualitative and quantitative analysis when there is a mismatch between analysis resources and the problem. This can result in elaborate analysis of trivial data or inadequate analysis in a complex problem of major concern. The researcher must remember the intent of the study and regularly weigh choices and options against two factors: available resources and the value of that new information.

In some respects, beginning the focus group analysis is like standing at the entrance of a maze. Several different paths are readily apparent at the beginning, and as the traveler continues, additional paths and choices continually emerge. It is unknown to the traveler if the path will be productive until it has been explored, but the process of exploration requires an investment of effort even if it is just a peek around the corner. Survival requires a clear fix on the purpose of the study.

WHAT MAKES QUALITATIVE ANALYSIS COMPLEX?

Consider the distinction between analysis of words and analysis of numbers. Analysis of numbers can be seductive. It is seductive in the sense that the researcher gains a sense of accomplishment and confidence by knowing exactly the nature of the results. The results of quantitative inquiry come out the same each time the analysis is replicated—if they don't, it's time to fix the computer. Moreover, analysis procedures are firmly grounded in research traditions. In quantitative analysis, the respondents select numbers that best represent their position on a measurement scale. The researcher assumes that the scale and the question are appropriate instruments to measure the phenomenon being considered. Unfortunately, elaborate statistical procedures cannot compensate for ambiguity in questions or responses.

Some survey results consist primarily of numbers because the respondent is requested to select a number on a scale that represents his or her point of view. The number then becomes a symbol of reality and the basis of analysis. The researcher might not know if the respondent really understood the question or if the available response choices were applicable or appropriate for the individual. In some situations, the respondent might find that none of the response choices is exactly on target or that the choices apply only in certain situations. When these situations occur, the reliability of the results are jeopardized. The survey researcher will often attempt to eliminate these factors by pilot testing the instrument; nevertheless, surveys that reduce reality to numbers will have inherent flaws in communication—some more than others. This does not mean that we should abandon statistical analysis, but rather we should recognize inherent assumptions and treat all data that measure human experiences with adequate humility.

Focus groups present another face of reality in that open-ended questions allow the participants to select the manner in which they respond. Furthermore, focus groups encourage interaction among the respondents and allow people to change their opinions after discussion with others.

The complexity of focus group analysis occurs at several levels. When a question is asked, two people will answer using different words. The analyst needs to consider how to compare the different answers. Analysis begins with a comparison of the words used in the answer. Are the words identical, similar, related, unrelated? For example, if the words are similar, then the analyst needs to consider other factors as well. What was the context of the comments? Were the two respondents really talking about the same thing when they answered? Did the discussion evolve so that the second respondent was keying his response to a different example? Also, the researcher must consider the emphasis or intensity of the respondent's comment. Another consideration relates to the internal consistency of the comments. Did respondents change their position later in the discussion? Still another consideration relates to the specificity of the responses in follow-up probes. Were the respondents able to provide examples or elaborate on the issue when probed? Clearly, the researcher must take multiple dimensions into consideration when comparing apparently similar responses.

The analysis process is like detective work. One looks for clues, but, in this case, the clues are trends and patterns that reappear among various focus groups. The researcher's task is to prepare a statement about what was found, a statement that emerges from and is supported by available evidence. In preparing the statement, the researcher seeks primarily to identify evidence that repeats and is common to several participants. Some attention, however, is also placed on determining the range and diversity of experiences or perceptions. The researcher must identify those opinions, ideas, or feelings that repeat even though they are expressed in different words and styles. Opinions that are expressed only once are enlightening but should not form the crux of the report.

THE CONCEPT OF ANALYSIS

The Role of the Analyst:
The Analysis Continuum

An area of concern early in the analysis process revolves around the analytical role of the researcher. A helpful way of thinking about this role is to consider a continuum of analysis ranging from presentation of raw data to interpretation of data.

The Analysis Continuum
Raw data ←→ Descriptive Statements ←→ Interpretation

On one side of the continuum is the presentation of raw data—the exact statements of focus group participants as they responded to specific topics in the discussion. These statements might be ordered in categories that are of concern to the client. For example, the statements might be ordered on the level of support (from very supportive to not at all supportive), or on the age of the respondents (responses from participants in their twenties, thirties, forties, and so on). Another option is to place the responses in categories by participant characteristics (occupational categories, gender, relationship to the program, and so on).

Midway on the continuum are descriptive statements—summary statements of respondent comments. When using this style, the researcher sets out to provide a brief description that is based on the raw data followed by illustrative examples of the raw data. While the presentation of raw data usually involves including all responses, the descriptive style seeks to simplify the task of the reader by providing typical or illuminating quotes.

The decision of which quotes to include sometimes presents a problem to the researcher. The selection choice should be influenced by the purpose of the study. If the study intends to describe the range and diversity of comments, then examples should be selected with this in mind. At other times, the purpose is to provide insights into typical, common, or usual ways in which participants respond, and, if so, the researcher should not include quotes that are unusual.

Interpretation is the most complex role for the researcher. The interpretative side of the continuum builds on the descriptive process by presenting the meaning of the data as opposed to a summary of the data. While the descriptive process results in a summary, the interpretative process aims to provide understanding.

Here's an example to illustrate the interpretative process. Several years ago, the Minnesota Extension Service was considering offering a computer course for farmers. After conducting a series of focus groups, the idea was scrapped. In a variety of ways, farmers were saying the same thing—they were impressed with computers, but they felt they didn't have sufficient knowledge to operate the machines and software. After reviewing the comments, the analyst prepared the following interpretation: The farmers had a "fear of failure" relating to microcomputers. Farmers lamented the cost of computers, but they were used to large investments for other types of farming equipment. The fear that the farmers had was in making an investment in an unfamiliar piece of equipment. The phrase "fear of failure" was not specifically mentioned by any farmer; however, this theme was repeated throughout the discussion. In this situation, the researcher prepared an interpretation that enabled the reader to get quickly to the point.

Clearly, the interpretative role of analysis is more complex and difficult than either the presentation of raw data or the descriptions of findings. Interpretation takes into account evidence beyond words on a transcript and includes evidence from the field notes. In addition, it also considers the intensity of participant comments, specificity of examples, and consistency of statements by respondents.

SYSTEMATIC AND VERIFIABLE PROCESSES

The analysis process must be systematic and verifiable. It is systematic in the sense that it follows a prescribed, sequential process. The analysis must also be verifiable—a process that would permit another researcher to arrive at similar conclusions using available documents and raw data. There is a tendency for novice researchers to see selectively only the aspects of the discussion that confirm their particular point of view. Our history with the topic, our expectations of what participants might say, and our personal opinions all work together to create a noisy environment for analysis. The researcher must filter out preconceptions, expectations, and personal opinions and tune in to the signals being transmitted by participants. Often, the researcher will go into the discussion with certain hunches of how participants might feel. Consequently, the researcher tends to look for evidence to support these hunches and overlook data that present different points of view. Mueller (1987, p. 5) recounts an example:

The first set of focus group interviews I conducted was with farm couples in northwestern Minnesota. My colleague and I were attempting to learn more about farm family perceptions of University programs for large scale producers. In the course of the interviews farm business decision making was often discussed, both husband and wives making statements about bookkeeping, banking and loan application responsibilities. When my colleague and I analyzed our interviews, he concluded that most financial decisions were "still" made by the farmer. It took several minutes of reviewing quotes and summary notes before he was convinced of the contrary. My colleague grew up on a Minnesota farm, with his father making most farm financial business decisions. He was selectively attending to comments which supported his previously held notions about farm families.

In this case, the systematic and verifiable procedures assisted the moderator team in placing the comments in perspective, separating out the personal bias of past experiences, hunches, or expectations.

THE ANALYST

Ideally, the moderator or assistant moderator should also do the analysis, if at all possible. These individuals have had firsthand exposure to each of the discussions, have observed the interactions of all participants, and likely have had the most intensive exposure to the problem at hand.

In some situations, such as when nonresearchers are recruited to moderate, the moderator may not have the analytic skills or time required to perform the analysis. Analysis of focus groups does require special skills different from the skills of moderating and requires a disciplined effort that some moderators may not possess. It is possible to separate the moderating and analysis functions and have each task performed by different individuals. Exercising this option requires careful planning and precise definition of tasks. At times, this division of labor is the preferred option.

For example, in some organizations, the professionals coordinating the research effort may be too well known or associated with certain issues by the participants of focus groups to be effective moderators. It is akin to a clergyman asking church members on Tuesday if they are following the precepts of Sunday's sermon. In these cases, a proxy can be identified and trained to moderate the discussions and begin the analysis process. The later, complete analysis could then be conducted by the professional responsible for the research effort or by focus group experts outside of the organization who are skilled in qualitative analysis. In these situations, it is necessary for the research director to specify the questioning route, arrange for the careful training of moderators, identify procedures for collecting data, and conduct a group debriefing of all moderators.

THE CHRONOLOGICAL
SEQUENCE OF ANALYSIS

The analysis process begins during the presession small talk. The moderator is observing the levels of familiarity between participants. If several people are related, well acquainted, or work together, this factor needs to be considered in the later analysis.

As soon as participants have left the discussion location, the moderator and assistant moderator should retreat to a quiet location. They first spot-check the tape recorder to ensure that it captured participant comments. By using "fast forward" and "play" at several places in the tape, it is possible quickly to determine if the tape has sufficient clarity and volume to be usable for later more detailed analysis. If the tape cannot be salvaged, the moderating team may want to reconstruct the discussion immediately, as best they can from memory and notes. If the tape is acceptable, then the moderating team can begin the postmeeting discussion.

It may be helpful to tape-record this debriefing. Also, it is helpful to write down summary comments, and, soon after, listen to the complete tape to write a more complete summary of the discussion. This written summary should be prepared within hours after the session and preferably before the next focus group. At times, researchers are tempted to schedule focus group sessions back-to-back to achieve efficiency, but this should be avoided until the researcher is thoroughly familiar with the focus group procedure. Inadequate time between sessions can jeopardize the quality of the analysis.

The purpose of the debriefing is for the moderator and assistant moderator to compare notes. This process can occur in several different ways. A few moments of silent reflection can be beneficial. This should be followed by a sharing of observations. During this discussion, the moderator team might begin by talking about participant responses to the key questions. The intent of this discussion is to arrive at a short summary, mutually agreeable to both team members, that would describe the findings and interpretation of the key issues in the study. If the moderator and assistant moderator disagree on certain issues, then both points of view should be cited for later, more careful examination. During this debriefing, it is helpful to be certain that field notes captured information on

— changes in the questioning route
— participant characteristics
— descriptive phrases or words used by participants as they discussed the key question
— theme in the responses to the key questions
— subthemes indicating a point of view held by participants with common characteristics (i.e., seniors agreeing on a similar perceptions, but not necessarily others within the group)
— descriptions of participant enthusiasm

—consistency between participant comments and their reported behaviors
—body language: information obtained by observing body movements (head nodding, indication of boredom, frustration, anxiety, and so on)
—new avenues of questioning that should be considered in future focus groups: should questions be eliminated, revised, or added?
—the overall mood of the discussion (i.e., were participants eager to discuss and self-energized?)

Brief summary reports of the discussion should be completed as soon after the discussion as possible. We have difficulty remembering distinctions among focus groups. For this reason, brief written reports using the raw data (field notes and tapes) are essential. This preliminary analysis is completed when a short written summary of a discussion is completed.

The analysis process then continues by gathering together brief summary reports, tape recordings, questioning route, demographic information about the participants, and, if available, transcripts of the discussion.

(1) The researcher reads all the summaries at one sitting and makes notes of potential trends and patterns. Strongly held opinions and frequently held opinions are noted.

(2) If transcripts are available, the researcher then reads each transcript. In this first reading of the transcript, the researcher marks sections of the transcript that relate to each question in the questioning route. This enables the researcher to locate the responses to specific questions quickly when making comparisons across focus groups. The researcher also marks participant comments that may be worthy of future quotation. If the typist has not had previous experience in typing focus group interviews, it is often worthwhile to listen to the tape while reading the transcript. This process serves as a check to ensure that participants are correctly identified and that the statements are accurate and complete.

(3) The researcher listens to the tapes or reads the transcripts concentrating on one issue or question at a time. After all responses to a question have been examined, the researcher prepares a brief summary statement that describes the discussion. Attention is placed on identifying the themes or patterns across the groups as well as themes that relate to respondents with similar demographic characteristics.

When conducting this analysis the researcher gives consideration to five factors:

(a) Consider the words. The researcher should think about both the actual words used by the participants and the meanings of those words. A variety of words and phrases will be used and the researcher will need to determine the degree of similarity between these responses. At times, the researcher might make a frequency count of commonly used words, cluster similar concepts together, or arrange the responses on a continuum or in categories.

(b) Consider the context. Participant responses were triggered by a stimulus—a question asked by the moderator or a comment from another participant. The researcher should examine the context by finding the triggering stimulus and then interpret the comment in light of that environment. For example, when the moderator asks an open-ended question, the first participant begins recounting a specific experience. These comments then provide a stimulus for the second respondent who may overlook the larger issue and respond to a narrow aspect of the original question. In other situations, the second participant might be triggered by the extreme comments of an earlier speaker and deliberately and carefully attempt to provide a degree of balance in the discussion. Also, the context can change when the moderator asks a question a second time in slightly different words.

The context depends not only on the preceding discussion but also on the tone and intensity of the oral comment. The discussion transcript greatly assists the researcher in the analysis, but this written summary has an inherent limitation. The tone and inflection of the comment might be interpreted in one way when heard in a group setting and in another way when read in a transcript. For example, suppose several respondents had responded to a question with exactly the same words but with variations in emphasis on certain words.

Comment	*Translation*
"This was GOOD!"	(It was good.)
"This was GOOD?"	(It was supposed to be good, but wasn't.)
"THIS was good!"	(This one was good, others were not.)
"This WAS good."	(It used to be good, but not anymore.)

(c) Consider the internal consistency. Participants in focus groups change and sometimes even reverse their positions after interaction with others. This phenomenon rarely occurs in individual interviews due to a lack of interaction from other participants. When there is a shift in opinion, the researcher typically traces the flow of the conversation to

determine clues that might explain the change. The shift is noted and may take on importance in the final report if opinion shifts are relevant to the purpose of the study.

(d) Consider the specificity of responses. Responses that are specific and based on experiences should be given more weight than responses that are vague and impersonal. To wh. 't degree can the respondent provide details when asked a follow-up probe? Greater attention is often placed on responses that are in the first person as opposed to hypothetical third-person answers. For example, "I feel the new practice is important because I have used it and been satisfied" has more weight than "These practices are good and people in the area should use them."

(e) Find the big ideas. The researcher can get so close to a multitude of comments and details that trends or ideas that cut across the entire discussion are missed. One of the traps of analysis is not seeing the big ideas. It may be helpful to take a few steps back from the discussions by allowing an extra day for the big ideas to percolate. For example, after finishing the analysis, the researcher might set the report aside for a brief period and then jot down three or four of the most important findings. Assistant moderators or others skilled in qualitative analysis might review the process and verify the big ideas.

At times, the researcher might find an unanticipated big idea that provides insight into how the consumer views the product or service. Big ideas emerge from an accumulation of evidence—the words used, the body language, the intensity of comments—rather than from isolated comments. Look for the big ideas not only in the responses to key questions but throughout the discussion.

(4) Consider the purpose of the report. The researcher should reflect back on the objectives of the study and the information needed by decision makers. The type and scope of the final report will guide the analysis process. For example, focus group reports typically fall into three categories: (a) brief oral reports that highlight key findings, (b) descriptive reports (oral and/or written) that summarize comments or observations of participants, and (c) analytical reports (oral and/or written) that highlight key trends or findings and also include selected comments as examples.

SUGGESTIONS FOR DATA REDUCTION

The analyst faces a challenge of data reduction. The amount of data collected in focus group discussions is considerable. A transcript from one focus group can easily consist of 20 single-spaced pages. In a typical situation, the researcher is confronted with 80 pages of single-spaced transcripts, eight hours of tape, and field notes from four discussions. The complexity of the task can be overwhelming. The ideal solution would be for the analyst to have an excellent memory, capable of storing all details and retrieving the correct data just when needed. Unfortunately, due to limited memories, researchers must rely on other strategies to assist in the analysis process. In order to cope with this complexity, researchers often use one or more of the following implements: tape recorders, word processors, and transcripts along with scissors or colored marking pens.

Variable speed tape players save valuable time. In the past few years, a new type of cassette tape recorder has entered the market. It enables the researcher to play back the tape at various speeds. The recorder can be sped up to almost twice the normal speed with minimal distortion or slowed down to about 75% of normal speed to capture the exact words of a critical participant comment. The variable speed tape recorder costs a bit more than the standard cassette recorder but is well worth the extra investment.

Cassette players with double decks are helpful in transferring sections of one tape onto another tape. The advent of reasonably priced double deck cassette players enables the researcher to listen to a tape and then make a copy of selected relevant comments on the second tape deck. If needed, all responses to a particular question can be packed in one place on the second tape. This process enables the researcher to play all responses to one question without changing cassettes. A strategy that I prefer is to use the double deck recorder to capture a collection of the most insightful quotes from participants. This second tape with selected quotes has proven to be helpful evidence in oral reports. The double deck recorders are also helpful in making a backup copy of tapes.

Some researchers prefer using word processors to type significant quotes while listening to the cassette tape. The word processor offers several advantages over a typewriter in that the researcher can later sort, categorize, and rearrange statements with ease. In addition, the computer provides the opportunity for using data base filing software to sort comments by respondent characteristics.

A low-technology option involves the use of scissors or colored marking pens on transcripts. If entire transcripts of the discussion are available, the researcher can cut out or mark sections that relate to specific themes for later aggregation.

ANALYSIS ISSUES TO CONSIDER

When undertaking the analysis, the researcher will need to think about several issues, including transcribing the tapes, the use of quotations, and nonverbal communication in the groups.

Transcribing Versus
Relistening to the Tapes

When resources permit, it is preferable to have the tapes transcribed before beginning the analysis. Unfortunately, it usually takes at least a full day of secretarial time to transcribe a two-hour focus group session. This step may not be practical if many groups have been held or if secretaries are already overloaded. Transcripts offer a major advantage in speeding up the process of sorting and categorizing and in enabling others to verify the analysis more quickly.

Editing Messy Quotations

People do not talk in nice crisp statements that result in insightful quotations. In real life, people use incomplete sentences or ramble along with disconnected thoughts strung together with verbal pauses. Thus transcripts of focus group interviews contain messy quotations. The researcher must determine the extent to which statements can be abridged or modified. Long quotes are often not read by readers, and, in some statements, only a portion is critical to capture the intent of the speaker. *The most important aspect in using quotations is that the researcher captures the intended meaning of the speaker.* Sometimes the actual words do not convey the meaning—as in situations where the speaker is trying to use humor and will say the opposite of what is intended. The researcher has an obligation to present the views of the participants fairly and accurately. In order to fulfill this obligation, some minor editing to correct grammar is appropriate as long as the meaning is not changed.

Nonverbal Communication in
the Focus Group

Some types of nonverbal communication are often overlooked in the analysis, especially when the researcher relies only on transcripts. The researcher should consider the energy level or enthusiasm within the group. Enthusiastic comments and excitement for the topic should be factored into the statements of findings. Also note the degree of spontaneity and the extent of participant involvement. Spontaneous comments, where probing is not needed, may signal that people are interested in the idea. In addition, the researcher should be attentive to the body language expressed during the group session. The moderator and assistant moderator should make notes of the nonverbal responses during the actual interview session, which are then considered when analyzing the results.

**The Use of Numbers in
Focus Group Results**

Numbers and percentages are not appropriate for focus group research and should not be included in the report. Numbers convey the impression that results can be projected to a population, and this is not within the capabilities of qualitative research procedures. Instead, the researcher might consider the use of adjectival phrases such as "the prevalent feeling was that . . ." or "several participants strongly felt that . . ." or even "most of the participants agreed that . . . ."

SUMMARY

In review, remember that the researcher is the detective looking for trends and patterns that occur across the various groups. The analysis process begins with assembling the raw materials and getting an overview or total picture of the entire process. The researcher's role in analysis covers a continuum with assembly of raw data on one extreme and interpretative comments on the other. The analysis process involves consideration of words, tone, context, nonverbals, internal consistency, specificity of responses, and big ideas. Data reduction strategies in the analysis are essential. Finally, and most important, analysis of focus group results must be systematic and verifiable. It is a careful and deliberate process of examining, categorizing, and tabulating evidence, and it is not hunches, guesses, or whatever one wants it to be.

APPENDIX:
FOCUS GROUP ANALYSIS TIPS

Materials Needed

A copy of the questioning route
Copies of all transcripts
Tapes of all interviews
Demographic information about the respondents
Copies of moderator and assistant moderator summaries or notes

(1) Read all summaries at one sitting. Makes note of potential trends and patterns. Strongly held opinions and frequently held opinions are also noted.

(2) If transcripts are available, read each transcript. Mark sections of the transcript that relate to each question in the questioning route. Mark participant comments that may be worthy of future quotation.

(3) Examine one question at a time. Concentrate on one issue or question at a time. After all responses to a question have been examined, prepare a brief summary statement that describes the discussion. Attention is placed on identifying the themes or patterns across the groups as well as themes that relate to respondents with similar demographic characteristics.

When Conducting This Analysis

(a) Consider the words. Think about both the actual words used by the participants and the meanings of those words. A variety of words and phrases will be used and the analyst will need to determine the degree of similarity between these responses. The researcher might consider conducting a frequency count of commonly used words, clustering similar concepts together, or arranging the responses on a continuum or in categories.

(b) Consider the context. Participant responses were triggered by a stimulus—a question asked by the moderator or a comment from another participant. Examine the context by finding the triggering stimulus and then interpret the comment in light of that environment.

The context depends not only on the preceding discussion but also on the tone and intensity of the oral comment. The discussion transcript greatly assists the researcher in the analysis, but this written summary has an inherent limitation. The tone and inflection of the comment might be interpreted in one way when heard in a group setting and in another way when read in a transcript.

(c) Consider the internal consistency. Participants in focus groups change and sometimes even reverse their positions after interaction with others. This phenomenon rarely occurs in individual interviews due to a lack of interaction from other participants. When there is a shift in opinion, the researcher typically traces the flow of the conversation to determine clues that might explain the change. The shift is noted and may take on importance in the final report if opinion shifts are relevant to the purpose of the study.

(d) Consider the specificity of responses. Responses that are specific and based on experiences should be given more weight than responses that are vague and impersonal. To what degree can the respondent provide details when asked a follow-up probe? Greater attention is often placed on responses that are in the first person as opposed to hypothetical third-person answers. For example, "I feel the new practice is important because I have used it and been satisfied" has more weight than "These practices are good and people in the area should use them."

(e) Find the big ideas. The researcher can get so close to a multitude of comments and details that trends or ideas that cut across the entire discussion are missed. One of the traps of analysis is not seeing the big ideas. It may be helpful to take a few steps back from the discussions by allowing an extra day for the big ideas to percolate. For example, after finishing the analysis, the researcher might set the report aside for a brief period and then jot down the three or four of the most important findings. Assistant moderators or others skilled in qualitative analysis might review the process and verify the big ideas.

At times, the researcher might find an unanticipated big idea that provides insight into how the consumer views the product or service. Big ideas emerge from an accumulation of evidence—the words used, the body language, the intensity of comments—rather than from isolated comments. Look for the big ideas not only in the responses to key questions but throughout the discussion.

(4) Consider the purpose of the report. Reflect back on the objectives of the study and the information needed by decision makers. The type and scope of the final report will guide the analysis process. For example, focus group reports typically fall into three categories: (a) brief oral reports that highlight key findings, (b) descriptive reports (oral and/or written) that summarize comments or observations of participants, and (c) analytical reports (oral and/or written) that highlight key trends or findings and also include selected comments as examples.

8

Reporting Focus Group Results

Reports do make a difference! Research results are sometimes ignored because of inadequate or ineffective reporting. At times, researchers have underestimated the importance of oral and written reports. In part, this may be due to traditions within the academic community. Traditionally, academic researchers have prepared reports for others within the research community but not for those who make day-by-day decisions within organizations. Their reports have thus often focused on uncovering theories, principles, and truths to guide future researchers. In an academic environment, reports are assessed by the degree of adherence to appropriate research methodology, rigor, and generalizability.

One professional group that has been concerned about reporting has been evaluators. In the last several decades, evaluators have been troubled about the lack of use and misuse of evaluation results. This attention to using results is grounded in the *Standards for Evaluation* as prepared by the Joint Committee on Standards for Educational Evaluation (1981). The Joint Committee underscored the importance of evaluation utility—that is, the potential for "an evaluation to serve the practical information needs of given audiences." The *Standards* emphasized the need for clarity, dissemination, and timeliness. In effect, the *Standards* recognized that evaluations are to be useful to specific people for specific purposes and not merely as academic exercises that add to our existing body of knowledge.

A second professional group, market researchers, have had a rich tradition in applied research and have for a number of years placed emphasis on research results that assist decision makers. In this profession, the research effort has been designed from the beginning to produce information related to specific decisions. For example, market researchers attempt to answer, Should we introduce the new product?

Will the new product be purchased? What strategies should be used in advertising the product? Both professions, evaluation and market research, have contributed to our ability to communicate findings of research efforts, and this chapter draws on the methods of both disciplines that are relevant to focus group interviewing.

CONSIDER THE AUDIENCE

A Tale

Once upon a time there was a special kingdom. A wise king ruled this vast kingdom. Throughout the week the king would consider the needs and problems of the realm, and make weekly pronouncements, laws, and decrees intended to address his subjects' concerns. The wise king grew weary of his awesome responsibility, because his solutions didn't always work and he suspected that his weekly pronouncements were in fact weakly pronouncements.

The king was indeed wise, and decided to consult his royal advisers before decisions were announced. The royal court was ablaze with excitement and eagerly did all members provide advice to the king. Knights and wizards, ladies in waiting and ladies not waiting all provided counsel to the king. The king was pleased for the advice was helpful, and the king grew in stature and respect among his people.

One day, when considering a particularly important decision, the king's advisers recommended a special study which would be conducted by the royal researcher. This study would give the advisers the information they could use to help the king make the right decision. It was an important study that required much effort. Fortunately the royal researcher was trained in all of the latest techniques. The royal researcher was eager to oblige, and hastily retreated to examine the problem in more detail. The royal researcher had a special ivory tower where he practiced his craft and none had ever entered this ivy covered structure, except for royal research assistants. After four weeks the royal researcher came out of the tower with a comprehensive report.

The report was beautiful to behold for it had gold edges, sandalwood covers, and pages of the finest royal parchment. However, after reading the report the king and the royal advisers became troubled because the report was not useful. It was an elegant report, but it did not provide useful answers to the difficult decisions encountered by the king and royal court. The wise king then decreed that henceforth all royal researchers must "Consider the Information Users."

Modern-day kings, royal courts, and royal researchers face the same situation. Information is needed, but, all too often, what is produced is not specifically related to the problem at hand, has not involved the appropriate individuals, or is too late to be helpful. Those who plan research endeavors, including focus groups, should remember the royal decree: "Consider the Information Users."

The researcher begins his or her reporting efforts by reflecting on the audience—those who will be receiving and using the report. One of the pitfalls of reporting is fuzzy audience identification. Researchers have a tendency to write reports for amorphous groups—the organization, the feds, the board—as opposed to specific people. A helpful strategy is to reflect back on the identified users and assemble information of particular interest to these individuals. In some situations, different reports can be prepared for different uses, with each report emphasizing areas of concern and interest to each user category.

Those who prepare reports tend to assume that people prefer to learn about results in the same way that the researcher prefers. This assumption is in conflict with what is known about individual learning preferences. Evidence suggests that people differ on how they prefer to receive information. This leads us to two implications for researchers. First, they should learn as much as they can about their audiences' preferences in receiving information. Educational level, occupation, age, and other demographic data can be helpful in this inquiry. Often, the most insightful way to obtain this information is to inquire about the most memorable reports the user audience have received in the past. You might ask: What were these reports like? What took place? What about the report did you find especially helpful? The second implication is the necessity of using a variety of media. Reports can be prepared for presentation in a variety of ways: in writing or orally, or complimented with visuals, charts, photographs, audio/video tapes, tables or figures, just to name some of the options. The procedures used are limited only by resources and creativity. Reports with multiple media help ensure that the message is effectively communicated because the combination of methods accommodates individual learning preferences and also provides reinforcement of the findings.

When preparing reports for specific people, the emphasis is on clarity and understanding. As a result, the writing style is characterized by less formality, shorter words, and familiar vocabulary. Active voice is preferred to passive construction. Quotations, illustrations, or examples of concepts are encouraged. When writing for nonresearchers, the complex descriptions of analysis and technical jargon actually inhibit understanding. This is especially a temptation for university faculty who may wish to demonstrate their academic acumen to their professional colleagues. Complex research procedures, if used, must be explained in an understandable way to those not acquainted with such procedures.

CONSIDER THE
PURPOSE OF THE REPORT

Effective reporting serves three functions. First and foremost, the report is intended to communicate results. The underlying principle of reporting is that the report communicates useful information to an identifiable audience for a specific purpose. This means that a variety of media may be required, clarity of reporting is essential, and attention must be placed on the individual information needs of a specific people.

Second, the process of preparing reports assists the researcher in developing a logical description of the total investigation. This function is most apparent in the preparation of written reports. Report writing is a disciplined effort that helps the researcher arrange the findings, conclusions, and recommendations in a logical sequence that can be subjected to peer review. This disciplined effort results in tighter logic, more precise statements, and an overall improvement in quality.

The third purpose of reporting is to provide a historic record of findings. While the report is intended to serve more immediate needs of audiences, it also can provide a longer-term reference for future studies and decisions. Concerns and problems often reemerge, the environment may change, the recommendations for improving the program may not work, and decision makers may have need for reexamining or even replicating an earlier study. Therefore, one of the purposes of the report is to provide a document that can be subjected to examination at some point in the future.

The Nature of Reporting

Focus group reports can be of three types: oral only, written only, or a combination of both oral and written. Whenever possible, the researcher should attempt to provide the report in a combination of modes, because each method offers unique advantages. Oral reports allow for questions, clarification, and the use of taped highlights or quotations. Written reports are well suited for distribution within an organization and are preferred when people are difficult to gather together. When oral and written reports are used together, the advantages are multiplied.

THE WRITTEN REPORT

Aside from being clear and logical, the written report must also look attractive. Poor quality printing, inadequate covers, and shoddy assembly convey undesirable impressions of the total research effort. If necessary, the researcher should seek assistance in editing the report for clarity and to be certain that there are no misspellings or grammatical mistakes. A recommended outline for the written report includes the following:

(1) Cover page. The front cover should include the title, names of people receiving or commissioning the report, the names of the researchers, and the date the report is submitted.

(2) Summary. The brief, well-written summary describes why focus groups were conducted and lists major conclusions and recommendations. The summary is often limited to two pages. It should be able to stand alone. Although this section is placed first in the written report, it is often the last part written.

(3) Table of contents. This section is optional and need not be included when the report is brief. The table of contents provides the reader with information on how the report is organized and where various parts are located.

(4) Statement of the problem, key questions, and study methods. In this section, the researcher should describe the purpose of the study and include a brief description of the focus group interviews. The number of focus groups, the methods of selecting participants, and the number of people in each focus group should be included.

(5) Results. Most often results are organized around key questions or big ideas in the focus group interview. The results can be presented by using only raw data, using descriptive summaries, or using the interpretative approach. Each of these is described later in this chapter.

(6) Limitations and alternative explanations. This section can be placed within the results category if it is brief. Limitations refer to those aspects of the study that limit the transfer of findings, and the use of procedures that prevent conclusive statements about the programs. At times, the findings can yield different interpretations of results, and these alternative explanations are contained in this section of the written report.

(7) Conclusions and recommendations. The conclusions pull together the findings into clear summary statements. Recommendations are optional and not automatically included in all focus group reports. The recommendations are future oriented and provide suggestions as to what might be done with the results. Sometimes they are expressed in very specific terms and in other circumstances they are more generally stated.

(8) Appendix. The final part of the written report is the appendix, which includes additional materials that might be helpful to the reader. For example, it is advisable to include the questioning route for the focus group and the screening questionnaire. Additional quotations may also be included in the appendix. Overall, the written report is intended to attract and hold the attention of readers.

**Begin the Written
Report with a Framework**

The skeleton or framework of the report is composed of the key questions that were asked or the big ideas that have emerged from the discussion. These questions and big ideas serve as the outline for the written report. They can be written using three different styles or models. The first style of presentation consists of the question or idea and is followed by all participant comments (the raw data model). The second style is a summary description followed by illustrative quotes (the descriptive model). The third style is a summary description with illustrative quotes followed by an interpretation (the interpretative model).

Here are examples of these styles from a series of focus group interviews with parents. The first example illustrates reporting of raw data. In this example, the researcher included all comments in the focus group and then arranged these into clusters or categories. The categories were selected by the researcher after reviewing all comments.

When appropriate, the comments can be arranged on a continuum such as degree of support, agreement versus disagreement, or intensity. This style of reporting has the advantage of providing the reader with the total range of comments; however, the sheer length of the resulting report may discourage careful reading. The raw data model of reporting is particularly appropriate in situations in which the researcher has limited experience (such as with volunteers), when the audience is interested in receiving all comments, or when a descriptive or interpretative report follows.

REPORTING EXAMPLE 1:
RAW DATA

**"What Do You Look for in a
Youth Organization?"**

Responses from parents included

Category 1: Quality of Leaders

Good leaders who can be a role model. (John, May 2)

The person in charge must be a good influence because children idolize their leaders. (Mary, May 2)

I would like my son in a youth organization that has a dedicated adult leader. My son needs to succeed in something other than school. I want him to have the feeling of accomplishment that comes with hard work. (Bill, May 2)

Leaders are the most important thing in a youth organization. I don't want a crank for a leader. (Esther, May 2)

I want an adult who is patient and kind to work with my kids. (Marge, May 3)

Good leaders can accept kids just as they are. These adults can have fun with kids. They can laugh with kids and enjoy the company of young people. (Sue, May 3)

When I drop my daughter off at the youth organization for the first time I watch what she does. If the leader brings her into the group and makes her feel welcome I know that is a good leader. (Richard, May 3)

I was in scouts when I was young and I still remember my scoutmaster. He had a sense of humor and always brought out the best in all of us. He always had time to listen to our problems. (Bob, May 3)

Category 2: Convenience

Low cost. I can't afford uniforms and costly trips. (Bill, May 2)

I've got four kids and I'm not going to run them to four different organizations. Either all the kids get involved in one organization or none at all. (Tom, May 3)

Any organization that we would consider must be convenient. We have certain family times and the group can't interfere with that. (Esther, May 2)

Both my wife and I work and we just don't have time to run both Jim and

Jessica, our two kids, to different organizations. The youth organization has to be close enough so that our kids can walk. (Bob, May 3)

Distance from our home. The organization needs to be within walking or biking distance of our house. (Marge, May 3)

Cost is somewhat of a factor. (Richard, May 3)

Category 3: Values

You know what is most important for me is to be certain that the other parents are like me. I mean, we must have the same values on things like drinking and drugs. (John, May 2)

A wholesome environment. I want my son to be around the good kids in the community. (Bill, May 2)

A chance to get exercise and be out of doors. (Mary, May 2)

My son needs to be in a group setting. He has troubles getting along with others and needs to learn to cooperate and compromise. (Marge, May 3)

The only group activity my children need is the church. Everything they need is within the church. (Sue, May 2)

Category 4: Other

My daughter needs to be able to do something she can feel good about and to have the opportunity to do well. She's not sports-minded and needs an opportunity to get recognition for her own talents. (Richard, May 3)

Lots of activities. I want my kid to be busy. You know what they say about idle hands. (Tom, May 3)

* * *

The next example is a descriptive summary. This style of reporting begins with a summary paragraph and then includes illustrative quotes. The quotes selected are intended to help the reader understand the way in which respondents answered the question.

REPORTING EXAMPLE 2:
DESCRIPTIVE SUMMARY

**"What Do You as a Parent Look for
in a Youth Organization?"**

In each group session, the parents cited a number of factors with two characteristics mentioned most often. These were the quality of adult leadership and the importance of convenience. Parents were concerned that their children were exposed to adults who understood and related well to youth. The issue of quality leadership was expressed in different ways, with attention placed more on the personal attributes rather than on the knowledge or technical expertise of the volunteer. In this community, the parents were also very concerned about youth organizations not getting in the way of family, employment, or other social commitments. Parents favored youth organizations that were convenient to their present life-style. Factors mentioned with lesser frequency related to the values of the youth organization and the opportunity for youth to achieve.

Typical comments by these parents included:

> The person in charge must be a good influence because children idolize their leaders. (Mary, May 2)

> Leaders are the most important thing in a youth organization. I don't want a crank for a leader. (Esther, May 2)

> I want an adult who is patient and kind to work with my kids. (Marge, May 3)

> Low cost. I can't afford uniforms and costly trips. (Bill, May 2)

> I've got four kids and I'm not going to run them to four different organizations. Either all the kids get involved in one organization or none at all. (Tom, May 3)

> Any organization that we would consider must be convenient. We have certain family times and the group can't interfere with that. (Esther, May 2)

The interpretative report builds on the descriptive report by the inclusion of a section on what the data mean.

* * *

REPORTING EXAMPLE 3:
INTERPRETATIVE

**"What Do You as a Parent Look for
in a Youth Organization?"**

In each group session, the parents cited a number of factors with two characteristics mentioned most often. These were the quality of adult leadership and the importance of convenience. Parents were concerned that their children were exposed to adults who understood and related well to youth. The issue of quality leadership was expressed in different ways, with attention placed more on the personal attributes rather than on the knowledge or technical expertise of the volunteer. In this community, the parents were also very concerned about youth organizations not getting in the way of family, employment, or other social commitments. Parents favored youth organizations that were convenient given their present life-style. Factors mentioned with lesser frequency related to the values of the youth organization and the opportunity for youth to achieve. Typical comments by these parents included:

> The person in charge must be a good influence because children idolize their leaders. (Mary, May 2)

> Leaders are the most important thing in a youth organization. I don't want a crank for a leader. (Esther, May 2)

> I want an adult who is patient and kind to work with my kids. (Marge, May 3)

> Low cost. I can't afford uniforms and costly trips. (Bill, May 2)

> I've got four kids and I'm not going to run them to four different organizations. Either all the kids get involved in one organization or none at all. (Tom, May 3)

> Any organization that we would consider must be convenient. We have certain family times and the group can't interfere with that. (Esther, May 2)

Parents were quite willing to discuss desirable features of a youth organization. Foremost among the features were factors relating to the adults in charge. Parents cited specific examples of desirable qualities that adult volunteers should have. Each parent had a notion of an ideal leader, which was based on some past experience either as a child or as an adult. Other features of the youth organization were subordinate to the quality of leadership in selecting an organization. The quality of leadership was the first factor cited in both focus groups. In addition, this characteristic surfaced repeatedly in both conversations. Parents believed that quality leadership was important for two reasons. It was necessary to maintain the interest of the youth, and, second, it provided the young people with a positive role model.

A secondary, but still important, characteristic of youth organizations related to the fit within the family structure. The organization had to be convenient to the family life-style most specifically in terms of time and cost demands.

* * *

The raw data reporting style is faster and easier for the researcher, but this style essentially transfers the work to the readers of the report. The raw data style is recommended only as a prelude to the descriptive or interpretative styles or in situations in which the analyst has limited skills or when the audience prefers reviewing all comments. Both the descriptive and the interpretative styles have the advantage of data reduction with the interpretative procedure providing the greatest depth in analysis.

THE ORAL REPORT

Before preparing the oral report, the speaker should find out how much time is available for the presentation, where the report will be given, and who the audience will be. Those receiving an oral evaluation report usually wish to discuss findings, respond to the results, or ask questions. The most successful oral reports have allocated only one-third to one-half of the time for the presentation and the remainder is spent in follow-up discussion. Therefore, a fifteen-minute report may include a five-minute presentation and ten minutes for questions, clarifications, and discussion of future action.

The first few minutes in an oral report are critical, and the speaker will need to set the stage quickly for the later findings. Often, the audience needs additional information as to why the study is important. The speaker should carefully lay out the framework describing why the study is important to the users. The oral presentation must be focused on the key points, citing the most important finding first, and then moving to less important findings. Within these first few moments, the speaker should highlight several key factors. For example, Why was the study needed? What do we know now that we didn't know before? or How can these finding be used? It is important to engage the audience quickly, to involve them in the report, to hook them into the study and explain clearly why the research effort was important.

When planning for the oral report, it is helpful to give consideration to the *ho-hum syndrome*, a typical reaction of elected officials. *Ho-hum* is best characterized by the questions going through the minds of the audience; for example, Do we really need this study? Don't we know this already? or Shouldn't this staff member be doing something really important instead of conducting these studies? To us, the results might seem enormously important with far-reaching implications, but to a busy elected official, they might sound like hair splitting and avoidance of real work. Much of what we discover in program evaluation and research efforts does tend to sound like common sense, and this tendency needs to be defused in the oral presentation. Often, the best procedure is to address it head-on by saying, "This study is of importance to us because ——————."

An outline for a written report does not transfer well to oral reporting. Often, researchers make the assumption that a report is a report, whether it be oral or written and that the sequence of information presented should be consistent in both kinds of reports. Oral reporting is different and it requires some special forethought and preparation. Some communications experts have recommended that the most important points be presented at the end of an oral presentation—that lesser points build toward the most critical point. This recommendation is helpful in a number of presentation environments, but it does not work well in evaluation or research reporting. Most reporting occurs in environments where people have time restrictions and limited patience, and where interruptions regularly occur. In these situations, brevity and conciseness are valued, and thus the most important findings are better placed at the top of the list.

A related issue concerns the number of points that should be included and the phrasing of those points. I have recommended that evaluators present oral reports with fewer than seven points. The basis of this recommendation stems from studies in cognitive psychology that suggest that five to seven items are the short-term memory capacity of most people. In addition, I have encouraged the use of short, active phrases to describe points as opposed to complete sentences. These brief phrases are designed to do two things: to convey the important concept and also to be easily remembered.

Visuals can effectively highlight the points. One useful tool is the briefing chart. These can be made on poster board or foam board and used to highlight key points. In addition, these charts should be reproduced in smaller 8×11 inch handouts and shared with the audience. Michael Hendricks (1984) has found charts with smaller handouts to be helpful in federal oral policy briefings. Selected quotations or even brief tape recordings of actual comments can also be very effective in the oral report, but they must be used in moderation.

Sometimes, the purpose of the oral report is unclear. I have observed the presentation of oral reports to organizations, and, when the reporter was finished, the group just looked at each other for a few awkward moments. This uncomfortable silence was then followed by some type of action typical of elected bodies. Someone usually moves that the report be approved or accepted. Then they can move on to really important matters. In these situations, the group receiving the oral report did not know why they were receiving the briefing simply because they were never told why it was being presented. At the end of the report, the reporter should indicate what action is recommended or why the report was presented, such as to provide a briefing, to form a study committee, to continue discussion at a later time, to seek funds to implement the findings, or to approve a new course of action. It is dangerous to assume that the audience will know what to do with the report.

Practice makes for better reports. The reporter should allow sufficient time to practice the oral report and to revise the written report after feedback from colleagues. Hastily prepared reports often have awkward construction, vague points, misspellings, and other aspects that limit their acceptance by users. In addition, the most qualified reporter should be selected to make the oral presentation. Some people have a natural or acquired talent for preparing written reports or presenting oral reports. Select the reporter by ability and not because of their role in the focus group interview. Naturally, the reporter will need to be sufficiently acquainted with both the process and the findings.

SUMMARY

In summary, not enough attention has been spent on communicating the results of our efforts. Reporting must be targeted to the audience and appropriate for the purpose of the study. Written reports begin with a framework that can include raw data, a descriptive summary, or an interpretative approach. One report may not be sufficient. The style of the report should match the capability of the analyst and the needs of the audience. Oral reports are structured differently from written reports with the most important point presented first. Audiences may need suggestions regarding how to respond, and the reporter should clearly indicate why the report is being presented.

APPENDIX A:
EXAMPLE OF A FOCUS GROUP REPORT
PREPARED FOR AN ACADEMIC MEETING

A Focus Group Report
on
Marketing Agricultural Education

by

Mary Anne Casey

Agricultural Education
320 Vocational Technical Education Building
1954 Buford Avenue
University of Minnesota
St. Paul, Minnesota
1986

Marketing agricultural programs is vital to land grant colleges. Fewer students are selecting agricultural programs, and, as a result, financial resources needed to sustain these educational programs are declining. Agricultural education departments within these land grant colleges are specifically interested in attracting more students. To market the agricultural education major effectively, it is necessary to develop a better understanding of what is appealing to prospective students. It is also important to find out more about the current image of the major and the college offering it.

Market researchers are using a state-of-the-art technique, focus group interviewing, to obtain clients' perceptions of products and services. People, purposefully selected, meet in small groups to discuss the products or services being studied. The interviewer or moderator raises various issues, focusing the discussion on topics of interest to the researcher.

The Agricultural Education Division of the University of Minnesota used this same market research technique to obtain information from prospective students. These students represented potential clients and held certain perceptions about our product, an agricultural education degree from the University of Minnesota. These perceptions greatly influenced the students' decisions concerning where to attend college and the course of instruction to pursue.

Colleges and other agricultural education providers that stay in touch with their clientele may be better able to adapt marketing strategies, curriculum, and services and thereby increase the number of students attracted.

PURPOSE AND OBJECTIVES

The purpose of this research effort was to obtain information to assist in marketing the agricultural education major at the University of Minnesota. Specific objectives of the study were

(1) to identify factors that influence students' decisions about the type and location of educational institution to attend beyond high school;
(2) to describe student perceptions of the University of Minnesota; and
(3) to describe students' perceptions of career opportunities available to agricultural education graduates.

STUDY PROCEDURES

Future Farmers of America (FFA) members in their junior year of high school from small rural schools attending the Minnesota State FFA Convention were the target population for the study. The study sought to determine the perceptions of this group for a number of reasons. FFA is a logical organization from which to recruit students, and it was assumed that FFA members attending the state convention were more likely to be prospective college students. Consequently, the researchers were particularly interested in perceptions and opinions of this group. Juniors were selected because it was felt that these students were at the age to be considering further education but probably would not have made specific plans to attend a particular institution.

Selected FFA advisers of small rural schools were asked to send one junior FFA member to a scheduled session. A 50% response rate was expected. Three sessions with an average of eight participants were conducted. Each session was conducted by a trained moderator, and, in two sessions, assistant moderators were present. Each session lasted about an hour and was audiotaped.

Questions used in the interviews were developed and reviewed by faculty members of the division of agricultural education. A pilot session was conducted with eight members of the Agricultural Education Club.

Each group was asked the same "core" list of questions (see the Appendix). General questions about organizations were used to begin the sessions, allowing each student a chance to talk and adjust to the group. The questions were designed to become more specific as the session progressed. Additional questions were asked as necessary to expand on an issue or probe into an area being discussed. A brief form was completed by participants during each session to encourage individual thought about attitudes toward occupations related to agricultural education before discussion.

Immediately after each session, moderators and assistant moderators noted common opinions and perceptions expressed by participants during the interview. Moderators and assistant moderators later met to discuss the interviews. Tapes were summarized and evaluated to detect reoccurring themes in the three sessions. A draft report of the analysis was prepared for review by members of the moderator team to check validity.

RESULTS

Reasons for Selecting an Institution

Students considered cost, size, and location the most important factors to consider when selecting a school. They also considered reputation of the school, recommendations of people, familiarity with the school, and how well they felt they would fit in.

Many students considering a four-year degree said they would go to a less expensive school (community college or state college) to take electives and then transfer to a more expensive school as juniors. Students generally did not consider the amount of financial aid or part-time work available from an institution when estimating costs. Size of the institution was important. Small schools were generally deemed more desirable than were larger institutions. Location was also a factor in their decisions. Institutions located close to home were more attractive to these students than were institutions of greater distance from their home communities. Student comments included the following:

> When you go to visit a college if the students are friendly, you kind of feel like you fit in. That helps a lot. If they look like you.

> I'm a junior this year but I'm going to college next year. I wanted to go to Crookston because it has a good reputation, and it's a good ag school. Since it is a small school you can get a lot of individual help and I really like that.

Perceptions of the
University of Minnesota

Students saw the University of Minnesota as "too big," "too scary," and "too impersonal." Its size, location, and perceived lack of humanistic qualities were deterrents to student enrollment. Students were concerned about the lack of personal attention available and the lack of opportunity for personal interaction. Students felt they would not have an opportunity to receive the help they would like at such a large institution. Rather than interpreting the large student body in a metropolitan area as an opportunity to meet more people, it was viewed as an obstacle to personal interaction. The reputation of huge class sizes and the huge student population led students to believe that they would have difficulties in getting to know other people. Students were also concerned that they might not "fit in" in a cosmopolitan setting. Students who had visited the campus before or had known someone who had attended the university were less apprehensive about the setting. Student comments included:

> I was looking at here and St. Cloud and I decided I'd go there for the first two years at least and then maybe I'd come here after I've gotten started. You know, the size of the classes, freshmen and sophomore years, its really scary.

> Its a big city and I wouldn't want to live in a big city.

> It seems a bit big. I know some people like that but I like to know a lot of people so if I say Hi to someone I know who I'm saying Hi to.

> Bigger classes with more kids, you wouldn't get to know a lot of people like you would at smaller schools.

Perceptions of Career Opportunities
Available to Ag Ed Graduates

The majority of these high school students were unaware of what a major in agricultural education was or for which occupations a graduate in agricultural education would be qualified. Those students who were aware of the major had a limited perception of the number of occupations available to agricultural education graduates.

CONCLUSIONS AND RECOMMENDATIONS

Students perceived the University of Minnesota as a large, impersonal institution and were concerned about their ability to succeed. Students wanted to attend an institution where teachers would be concerned about them. While these results may seem to be intuitively appealing, they were at odds with established procedures for recruiting students. Over the years, the university has portrayed itself as an institution with "4 million volumes in its library system," "great size," "44,000 students," and "250 undergraduate majors offered by 18 different colleges." (Prospective Student Brochure, 1985-1986)

With results from this study in mind, the agricultural education faculty reexamined its recruitment and marketing process, and made modifications. A revised recruitment plan was initiated that was specifically designed to alleviate anxieties of potential students. Letters sent to prospective students emphasized the smallness of the St. Paul campus, "about 3000 students," "friendly students," "a broad array of employment prospects," and "professors who really care." Recruitment techniques incorporating personal contact of prospective agricultural education students by either faculty or a faculty representative were seen as a positive way of overcoming some of the concern about lack of caring about the student at the university. The number of recruitment visits made to students was increased, and extra care was taken with students visiting campus to make them feel welcome.

This study reinforces the concept that students are consumers of higher education. Students are not blindly selecting institutions and programs by accident but rather after careful reflection. Even at the junior year of high school students exhibit specific preferences in their future educational goals. Agricultural education departments must remain in touch with these potential consumers and promote their programs in ways that attract and interest students.

Universities concerned about marketing their programs should consider using focus groups as a method of determining prospective students' current perceptions of their institutions and programs. Information obtained through focus groups can aid in decision making about how better to promote these institutions and their programs.

APPENDIX:
FOCUS GROUPS—MARKETING AGRICULTURAL
EDUCATION OUTLINE OF QUESTIONS

At the beginning of the session, students were asked to introduce themselves and name the youth organizations in which they participate.

(1) As we went around the room, I heard you mention several different youth organizations. In general, what influenced you to participate in these groups?

(2) All of you are members of FFA. What specifically influenced you to participate in FFA?

(3) Let's talk about educational opportunities after high school. A number of people anticipate training or education after high school. This education might be from an area vocational technical institute, a community college, a private college, a state university, or the University of Minnesota. The decision of where to go for more education can be influenced by a number of factors. What are the things that influence your choice?

(4) Some of you may be considering the University of Minnesota. What are the things about the university that impress you, specifically the things that might cause you to enroll at the university?

(5) What are the things that would cause you to stay away from the University of Minnesota?

(6) Some career areas are listed containing a number of different careers. In each cluster, put an M beside the career that strikes you as the most interesting and an L beside the career that seems least interesting or appealing. Circle the cluster of jobs that seem most interesting to you.

(7) What career categories are most interesting to you and what makes them interesting?

(8) Within the university or college, there are a number of departments. For example: chemical engineering, physics, history, and agronomy are just a few of the many departments. Another department is agricultural education. When you hear "agricultural education," what comes to mind?

APPENDIX B:
EXAMPLE OF A FOCUS GROUP REPORT
PREPARED IN TRADITIONAL FORMAT
FOR DECISION MAKERS

FEASIBILITY STUDY OF A
NEW EDUCATIONAL PROGRAM

"PROMOTION OF ISLAND GROWN VEGETABLES"

by

Rhoda M. Yoshino
County Extension Agent
Cooperative Extension Service
University of Hawaii
Spring 1987

SUMMARY

Hawaii has an abundance of locally grown vegetables, including choi sum, pak choi, and kai choi. These vegetables are an excellent value for the consumer due to low cost and high nutritional value, specifically because they are high in fiber and vitamins A and C. Increased consumption of these locally grown vegetables would benefit not only the consumers, but also the local vegetable industry. A strong vegetable industry in Hawaii would ensure longer-term availability at lower costs, and thereby benefit both consumers and producers.

The purpose of this study was to determine the feasibility of implementing a new educational program sponsored by the Cooperative Extension Service. The program, "Promotion of Island Grown Vegetables," would be designed to

(1) increase the consumer use of selected specialty vegetable varieties;

(2) improve consumer skills in selection, storage, and preparation of vegetables; and

(3) encourage an increase in the consumption of foods high in vitamin A and C and fiber.

The new program would be targeted to working homemakers. Program materials and delivery methods would focus on reaching homemakers in three different situations: (a) the work site, (b) the supermarket, and (c) the traditional Extension open meeting.

This study addresses only those programs intending to reach homemakers in the supermarket environment. Programs for the supermarkets are to be planned primarily as point of purchase materials: flyers with information on nutrition, selection, storage, and preparation; in-store demonstration. Volunteers will be recruited and trained as "Master Food Shoppers" to conduct the in-store demonstrations.

The strengths and weaknesses of the program format and delivery methods were assessed by two mini-focus group interviews. The audience was limited and targeted to the working homemaker. Fresh vegetable buying habits of homemakers were examined. The impact or lack of impact of the proposed program format and educational materials were assessed.

The findings indicated that the proposed format for the supermarket program needed to be modified. This format consisted of three components: recipes, nutritional place cards hung over the vegetable display, and in-store demonstrations conducted by trained "Master Food Shoppers."

The reactions of the homemakers to the format as originally planned were surprising. They rejected the recipes and nutrition information signs as not influencing their buying habits. They were very positive about the idea of trying food samples and watching the in-store demonstrations. Homemakers indicated that they would be influenced to buy the vegetables and make the recipe if the food tasted and smelled good.

Based on the findings of this study, the recommendations are to modify the format for the supermarket program to feature the in-store demonstrations as a primary method to influence homemakers to use locally grown specialty vegetable varieties. It would then be necessary to strengthen the "Master Food Shopper" program and to train more "masters" to conduct in-store food demonstrations. Recipe development should continue as support materials for handout at demonstrations. Nutrition information could be used during the demonstrations as visual aids.

BACKGROUND INFORMATION ON PROGRAM

New programs and program materials, in many instances, are developed and assumed to be successful based on the professional's best judgment and experience. Historically, new programs or materials have not been disastrous failures; however, the programs, materials, and delivery methods could have been examined and modified before implementation to ensure success without time delays and added cost of traditional trial and error methods. Determination of a new potential program's success prior to its implementation would greatly affect the use of the home economist's time and limited educational budget. On occasion, advisory groups have provided the home economist with program suggestions, but the opinions and comments of other clientele groups have not been systematically sought.

This project has provided an opportunity to target an audience and obtain opinions and comments from potential clients relative to the strengths and weaknesses of a new potential program before implementation. The focus group method has been selected as the primary tool to begin evaluating the feasibility of implementing the new program. Focus group discussions allow groups with similar characteristics to interact with each other and provide a range of responses relating to program strengths and weaknesses. The group setting encourages free flowing comments within a permissive environment. The individuals' common experiences and perceptions provide important clues to the possible success or failure of the new program. This study focused on the acceptability of the proposed delivery methods and format of the educational materials.

Two mini-focus groups were conducted. The first group (Group A) was made up of four homemakers and the second group (Group B) was made up of five homemakers. Both groups of homemakers were employed outside the home. All homemakers were female and prepared at least five meals for more than two people weekly. All the homemakers managed the food shopping weekly or biweekly.

A purposeful sample and the snowball method were used to identify participants for both groups. The homemakers in Group A all worked in the same medical office building but were from different offices. One homemaker attended a 30-minute lunchtime program on healthy snacks for preschool children conducted by the home economist about eight months earlier. The homemaker was asked for the name of a friend. The friend was screened using a list of questions and then invited to participate in the interview. The procedure was repeated until six homemakers were screened and invited to participate. Only four of the six participated in the interview. Homemakers ages ranged from 25 to 35 years old. All had children between one and ten years of age.

Group B began with a friend of a friend. As with the first group, each homemaker was screened and invited to participate in the discussion. Six homemakers were invited and five participated in the focus group. Homemakers' ages ranged from 45 to 48 years old. Four had children between 15 years to 24 years old. One had a parent and a sister living with her.

The Group A discussion was conducted during lunchtime in one of the homemaker's offices and took about an hour and a half. Group B met in a home in the evening and the discussion lasted about two hours. There was no attempt made formally to compensate the homemakers with money. Light refreshments were provided by the home economist for both groups.

The screening questionnaire to identify participants and the series of questions for the focus discussion were pilot tested with two home economists. The phrasing and the order of the questions were modified before use. The questioning route used in the focus group is included at the end of this report.

RESULTS

The Grocery Shopping Experience

Homemakers were asked to think back to the last time they went shopping. They were asked to consider: "How did you go about making your vegetable selections? What was important to you? What were you looking for? What factors influence your selection?"

All the homemakers from Group A stated that their family schedule greatly influenced the kind of meals they planned. During the week, they had meals that could be prepared in a short time or prepared in advance, such as spaghetti, chili, stew, or goulash.

All the homemakers stated that freshness and appearance of the vegetables were important. All the homemakers from Group A and two of the five from Group B made weekly menus and selected vegetables based on their menus. Three from Group A stated that they really didn't know how to select vegetables. Typical comments included

The vegetables have to look good or I won't buy them.

Appearance is real important. If it looks wilted, yellow or spotted, I'll change my menu and cook something else.

Sometimes I'll stand in front of a pile of potatoes and I'd say, "What would my mother look for?"

The general appearance of the vegetables and their freshness were important factors to the homemakers whenever they purchased vegetables. Although only the younger home-makers (Group A) indicated a lack of confidence in selecting vegetables, this could be an important negative factor affecting the young or inexperienced homemakers. Time was also another possible limiting factor affecting the kinds of meals prepared during the week.

Purchasing Leafy Greens

Homemakers were asked several questions about leafy green vegetables: "Do you buy leafy green vegetables, specialty vegetable varieties, such as choi sum or kai choi? When you buy these vegetables, which varieties do you select? What factors affect your selection?"

There were no consistent answers among the two groups. In Group A, only one homemaker bought these vegetables, two didn't know how to identify the vegetables or how to cook them, and one didn't have time to prepare the vegetables during the week. The responses of the homemakers in Group B were quite different. Their selections and frequency of use of the specialty varieties were influenced by price. Only one stated that she would buy the vegetables regardless of price if they looked good.

When the homemakers purchased these vegetables, they selected choi sum, kai choi, pak choi, and ung choi. A homemaker from Group A purchased choi sum weekly. Typical comments included:

> I buy the vegetables only if they're cheap or on special.
>
> I don't know what I'm buying. I need pictures of the vegetables, color pictures.
>
> Sometimes the signs are over two different vegetables and I don't know which is which.
>
> I would love to learn to prepare these vegetables. My husband would be so happy. The only time we eat them is when we eat Chinese food.

Of those homemakers who did purchase and use the specialty varieties, five of the six stated that price was a significant factor. Of the young group, half didn't know how to identify, select, or prepare these specialty varieties.

The Influence of the Family on Grocery Purchases

Participants were asked, "To what extent does family preference affect your buying habits?" Both groups stated that the family members greatly affected their selection of vegetables. Group A homemakers stated that their children were the key influence and their husbands in general would eat whatever they prepared. Group B homemakers agreed that their family's likes and dislikes of certain dishes determined their selections. They stated that they knew what their families would and wouldn't eat and also that they would try new dishes only on their husbands. Typical comments included

> I know what my family will eat.
>
> I'll buy certain vegetables when I have company and I know they will eat it.
>
> I'll try a new recipe on my husband, but never on my kids.
>
> My family judges every new recipe. They tell me if I keep the recipe or toss it.
>
> My son is a picky eater. He likes breakfast. You can't add too much vegetables there.

Family members exert a lot of influence on the buying habits of the homemakers. Homemakers are conscious of the likes and dislikes of their children and will buy and prepare food accordingly. In most cases, the spouse was willing to eat whatever was prepared.

The Influence of Nutritional Information on Grocery Purchases

Homemakers were asked about the influence of nutritional information when making vegetable purchases. The questions were as follows: When shopping for vegetables, are the nutrition information signs useful? Would the nutrition information influence you to buy one vegetable over the other?

In several of the supermarkets, nutritional signs were displayed over the vegetables. Information on vitamin and mineral content were given. Most of the homemakers did not use the information. Only three did not see the signs. A homemaker in Group A stated that nutrition information was important when she was selecting snacks for her children. A homemaker in Group B stated that nutrition information in general is important to her decision making but not in the store. Typical comments included

I would look at the signs, but it's more a matter of what I had last.

I always buy Manoa lettuce over iceberg because I know the vitamin A content is higher in Manoa.

The signs don't have any influence on me.

Of the homemakers who noticed the signs, no one used the information for making more nutritious selections. Nutrition information was important, but not in the immediate decision-making process in the store.

The Influence of Pictures on Grocery Purchases

Homemakers were asked whether a picture might influence their decision to purchase. The following question was asked: Would a picture of a prepared recipe, such as a picture of stir-fried vegetables in a wok, influence you to buy the vegetable and make the dish?

All the homemakers said no. One homemaker from Group A stated that if she was hungry, she would stop to look at the picture but generally would not buy the item unless it was on her list. Typical comments included

I don't look at the pictures.

When I'm hungry pictures influence me but I don't always buy the item in the picture.

I already have my mind made up, and I have my list. I try hard not to deviate from my list.

The homemakers were not interested in looking at pictures in the supermarket. Their decisions on what they would purchase were not influenced by pictures.

The Influence of Recipes on Grocery Purchases

The participants were asked about the influence of recipes: Would recipes placed in the produce area influence you to try a new vegetable? Where do you find new recipes?

In general, the homemakers from both groups stated that they would not pick up recipes in the grocery store or supermarket. Group B homemakers, because of their greater experience, did not "bother" with the recipes; only one indicated that she would look at the recipes if she had time. Group A homemakers said that the recipes had to be simple with few ingredients before they would take one. Then, after taking the recipe, they doubted if the larger recipe card would find its way into their recipe file. Three homemakers in Group A said they would not take recipes that were printed on a full-sized paper. Examples of the comments included

I don't even bother. I know what my family will eat.

I look through cookbooks or in magazines for new recipes.

Recipes have to be simple, like the ones on the soup can.

I need to see a color picture before I'll make the recipe. It has to look delicious.

I get my recipes from inserts in the electric bills and from the campaign brochures.

I always end up throwing away the recipes I collect in the supermarkets.

I won't try it unless I know what it tastes like.

The homemakers did not find it convenient to collect and transfer the recipes from the supermarket to their home files. It was evident that recipes were collected and reviewed during leisure time, not while shopping. If the recipe did appeal to the homemaker, it had to be in the proper format, or on cards, and not on a full-sized paper.

The Influence of In-Store Demonstrations on Grocery Purchases

The final set of questions related to the influence of in-store demonstrations. The following questions were asked: Remember the last time you were shopping and you came across a person demonstrating a product. Did you try the product? Did you buy the product? If the product tasted good, would you make the recipe for your family? Would you ask the demonstrator questions?

All the homemakers said they would sample the product. All said that they would stop and watch the demonstration for a while if they were not in a hurry. All said that if the product tasted good, they would buy it. Only Group B homemakers stated that they would go up and ask questions, but only if they had time. Among the comments were

If the product looked good, I would try it.

If the product smelled good, I would try it.

My kids will try it and if they like it, I'll buy it.

It's nice to know my baby will eat it.

If I don't see the demonstrator but I smell something good, I'll look up and down the aisles to find where the smell is coming from.

In-store demonstrations appeared to be a positive way to influence homemakers to try a new product. Though the dialogue between the shopper and the demonstrator was dependent on the time, there were positive responses to a person being available for questions.

LIMITATIONS

The study included small samples in two focus group interviews due to limited time constraints. Increasing the number of focus groups would provide more representative samples of targeted population groups. As a result, these findings should be considered exploratory and subject to later verification. While the small sample does limit the study, it does identify some consistent themes in the homemakers' selection of locally grown vegetables.

CONCLUSIONS AND RECOMMENDATIONS

The responses of both groups of homemakers provided important clues to the feasibility of implementing this program as planned. The homemakers' reactions to the program format and delivery methods were of particular interest. Based on their responses, both the program format and the delivery methods will need to be examined in greater detail.

The examination of the program strengths and weaknesses by lay groups was extremely beneficial. Market testing and focus group interviews were thought of only as marketing strategies used by advertising firms and supermarkets. The practical application was not transferred to the educational arena until this evaluation experience.

In spite of the limitations of the small sample, it was quite clear that the normal procedures of program planning and evaluation needed to be modified. The best judgment and experience of the home economist and the pilot testing of program materials with selected groups would not have been as effective in identifying the "bombs" (nutrition information and recipes) as were the mini-focus group interviews.

The findings from this study point to a need to modify both the delivery system and the format for the supermarket program. The in-store demonstrations were well received by both groups of homemakers. Demonstrations were originally considered to be a secondary promotion method to reinforce recipes and nutrition information. The proposed primary method, recipes and nutrition information, was almost totally rejected by both groups.

The unanticipated responses from both homemaker groups raise serious considerations regarding the "Master Food Shopper" program. The "Master" program will need to be examined in more detail, using, perhaps, focus group interviews. Recruitment procedures, selection of trainees, training program, and support will all need to be further scrutinized.

QUESTIONING ROUTE

(1) Think back to the last time you were shopping:

    (a) How did you go about making your vegetable selections?
    (b) What was important to you?
    (c) What were you looking for?
    (d) What factors, if any, affected your selection?

(2) Leafy greens:

   (a) Do you buy leafy green vegetables, specialty vegetable varieties such as choi sum, pak choi, kai choi?

   (b) When you buy these vegetables, what varieties do you select?

   (c) What factors, if any, affect your selection?

(3) Family preference:

   (a) To what extent do family preferences affect your buying habits?

(4) Nutrition information:

   (a) When shopping for vegetables, are the nutrition information signs useful?

   (b) Would nutrition information influence you to buy one vegetable over another?

(5) Pictures:

   (a) Would a picture of a prepared recipe such as a picture of stir-fried vegetables influence you to make the dish?

(6) Recipes:

   (a) Would recipes placed close to the vegetables influence you to try a new vegetable?

   (b) Where do you find new recipes?

(7) In-store demonstrations:

   (a) Remember, the last time you were shopping and you came across a person demonstrating a product. Did you try the product?

   (b) Did you buy the product?

   (c) If the product tasted good, would you make the recipe for your family?

   (d) Would you ask the demonstrator questions?

APPENDIX C:
EXAMPLE OF A SUMMARY FOCUS GROUP REPORT
PREPARED FOR DECISION MAKERS

The following report was prepared for the Chair of the Department of Rhetoric at the University of Minnesota and a planning committee for the annual Institute for Technical Communication (ITC). In previous years, the Institute had been offered for academics. The committee wanted to change the focus and design a program that would be of interest to practicing technical communicators as well as academics. Thus they commissioned a small market study of technical communicators from the Minneapolis-St. Paul area to gather information about their continuing education practices and needs.

MEMORANDUM

To: ITC Planning Committee
From: Sandra Becker
Re: Focus Group Report

As you requested, I have completed two group interviews of technical communicators from the Twin Cities area. Using the membership list of the Twin Cities' Society for Technical Communicators, I invited an equal mix of managers and nonmanagers as well as corporate and contract writers drawn at random. The uniformity of responses between the two groups seems to indicate that the results of the interviews are reasonably reliable.

The following information provided by the groups should help you make decisions about the program, pricing, and promotional tactics for next year's ITC. Based on those findings, I offer several recommendations for your consideration.

Findings

(1) Employers sponsored outside training opportunities for all respondents. Companies paid up to $200/day for courses that lasted up to three days. All of the courses were technical in nature.

(2) Courses longer than three days would not be well received by employers.

(3) Sponsorship and credibility of instructors, topics of training, timing, and location were the most important factors considered by potential participants. No single factor seemed more important than others.

(4) The following topics, in descending order of importance, were suggested as areas where employers weren't providing adequate training:

    (a) On-line documentation
    (b) Company politics, especially the role of the writer on the design team and within the company
    (c) Project management—scheduling, estimating, budgeting
    (d) Design, graphics, and graphics production
    (e) Product evaluation
    (f) The writer as teacher
    (g) Product liability and the technical writer.

Recommendations

(1) Keep the Institute less than four days. One of those days (or at least a half-day) could fall on a Saturday to demonstrate to employers the seriousness of the writers' desire to participate in the program. Keep the Institute in July as you have in the past.

(2) Charge over $100/pay given that the market will bear a $200/day fee if the topics are of interest to potential participants.

(3) Because both groups concurred about the topics listed above, I think you should incorporate as many of their suggestions as possible into the program.

(4) Use their language in your promotional materials. For example, instead of listing instructional design as a topic, use their phrase—*the writer as teacher*, or simply, *teaching*.

(5) Stress that the university is sponsoring the Institute and include some well-known experts on the program because sponsorship and expertise of presenters are considered important.

I would be happy to meet with your program subcommittee to provide additional information about the topics suggested by the respondents.

Part III

Issues and Concerns

The final section of this volume addresses three topics that are of particular concern to public and nonprofit organizations. Chapter 9 is an overview of how nonresearchers can effectively provide assistance in the focus group process. The robustness of focus groups is highlighted in Chapter 10, where variations of the discussion technique are described. Contracting for outside assistance with focus groups can be frustrating, so Chapter 11 offers helpful tips in getting hired help. Finally, what does the future hold for focus groups? The "Postscript" offers some factors on which the future of focus groups may depend.

9

Using Nonresearchers in Focus Groups

The nonresearcher may be one of the most valuable assets in conducting focus groups. By "nonresearcher," I am referring to everyone involved in the project except the researcher. Therefore, the term *nonresearcher* can include student help, employees not involved in research, and volunteers. Nonprofit organizations conducting focus group interviews can use the skills and talents of nonresearchers in a number of creative ways. The most common ways include advising on the study, assisting with specific functions, interpreting findings, and reporting results. Nonresearchers have effectively and successfully performed all of these tasks, in some cases better than professional researchers.

NONRESEARCHERS IN A TASK FORCE

Using nonresearchers in focus groups begins early; specifically, in the planning stage. Nonresearchers serving on an evaluation or research task force can provide valuable insights that can guide the entire study. The research task force is usually composed of three to seven individuals who represent varying interests and points of view. Members of the task force are either in the position of being able to use the results directly or are able to influence others who will be making decisions relating to the recommendations. The task force should include a mix of researchers and nonresearchers.

Patton (1982, p. 71) describes the purpose of the task force in the following manner:

> An evaluation task force is organized to make major decisions about the focus, methods, and purpose of the evaluation. The task force is a vehicle for actively involving key stakeholders in the evaluation. This helps

guarantee that the evaluation is relevant, appropriate, and useful. Moreover, the very processes involved in making decisions about an evaluation will typically increase the commitment of stakeholders to the utilization of evaluation results while also increasing their knowledge about evaluation, their sophistication in conducting evaluation research, and their ability to interpret evaluation findings. Finally, the task force allows the evaluator to share responsibility for decision making and utilization by providing a forum for the political and practical perspectives that best come from those stakeholders who will ultimately be involved in the utilization of evaluation results.

The challenge of using a task force is to tap the insights and strengths of the group in order to do what the group can do best, and to avoid activities that are too time consuming or inappropriate for group activity.

In my experiences with focus groups, we have found Patton's recommendation of four two-hour meetings with the research task force to be very workable. I have adapted these meetings slightly to include:

(1) Orientation to the study problem. The first session includes an overview of the problem from two perspectives. First, the researchers present the organizational perspective, and then, second, the task force members are encouraged to present their points of view. The intent of this first session is to identify the question(s) and discern which aspects of the problem are of greatest concern. To a degree, the first session provides an opportunity for the task force members to ventilate their personal points of view and to gain from the perceptions of others.

Between the first and second sessions, the chair of the task force develops the strategy for the next session, which includes an overview of options for collecting information. Note that the decision to use focus groups has not yet been made and focus groups should be considered along with other qualitative and quantitative procedures. I prefer to present several alternative plans sketched out in a draft, each alternative including a description of procedures, time lines, estimated resources, and an overview of the nature of the results. The chair of the task force or a staff member grounded in research procedures should be prepared to point out the advantages and disadvantages of each option.

(2) Consideration of alternative strategies. The second session begins with an overview of research strategies and allows the task force to consider which alternatives are preferable and why. If the task force favors using focus groups, then discussion should follow on issues relating to the composition of the focus groups and the role of

nonresearchers in the process. A brainstorming session might be conducted on possible questions that could be asked in the focus group sessions.

Following the second task force session, the research plan is finalized and instruments are identified. If focus groups are used, then the task force chair or research consultant will develop the questioning route based on the earlier brainstorming session with the task force. The research plan is fleshed out in greater detail, with attention to budgets and time constraints. Selected staff members within the organization might be requested to review the plan and questioning route and make suggestions for improvement.

(3) *Finalization of research procedures.* The third task force session is the final review prior to implementing the study. The chair or research consultant should review the details of the plan including the methods of selecting participants, incentives for participants, recruitment and training schedule for nonresearchers, and a review of the questioning route for the focus group. Often, it is helpful to conduct a pilot test of the focus group questions with the task force to determine if the questions flow smoothly and to elicit discussion and sharing of perceptions.

Following the third task force session, the research procedures are implemented. Focus groups are conducted and the results are analyzed.

(4) *Interpretation of results and recommendations.* The final task force session once again taps into the strengths of the committee members. They are asked to look over the results of the analysis and provide insights as to possible interpretations of results as well as recommendations. A dated preliminary draft (so marked) of the results is shared with the task force. The task force should be asked about their recommendations for reporting the results of the findings.

Following this final session, the final report is prepared, shared first with the members of the task force and then with other audiences.

NONRESEARCHERS ASSISTING WITH THE FOCUS GROUP PROCESS

Nonresearchers can be helpful in recruiting participants, moderating the focus group, preparing transcripts, and analyzing results. The researcher should consider the advantages and disadvantages of volunteers versus paid employees for each of these functions. The principle advantage of using volunteers is in cost savings, which for nonprofits can be a major factor. A secondary advantage is that some of these tasks enable volunteers to develop or enhance skills that can be transferred to other environments. The primary disadvantage is time—time to recruit and train volunteers of varying skill levels. Volunteers often require intensive training, and that training must fit into their schedules. The level of motivation among volunteers to complete their task may vary and conflicts in schedules often occur. In spite of these disadvantages, with proper recruitment, skillful supervision, and adequate training, volunteers can be helpful in the focus group process.

Volunteers can assist in recruiting focus group participants. The participants for a focus group must meet certain criteria relating to the purpose of the study, and when the criteria are quite specific, recruitment can be a major concern. For example, suppose a community church was considering starting a child-care service, a venture that had been suggested enthusiastically by mothers in the church. To make the project financially self-sufficient, the service would need to draw from families outside of the church membership. The child-care operation would require some investment for remodeling the building and purchases of equipment that would be, for all practical purposes, irreversible decisions. Prior to investing money in remodeling, the church might conduct a series of focus groups with mothers in the community. Focus groups would be designed to provide information about desirable specifications for child-care facilities as well as desirable and undesirable features of these kinds of services. The target audience for the focus groups might consist of working mothers between the ages of 25 and 40 who have children between the ages of one and five. In this example, the target audience is likely found in limited numbers in the community, and, furthermore, they are apt to be people with busy schedules who are reluctant to spend several hours at a meeting. The recruitment strategy might begin with the core of enthusiastic mothers. These mothers might become the volunteers needed to recruit other mothers into the focus groups, and, in addition, the volunteers may have helpful suggestions as to incentives for participation as well as means of getting in touch with mothers. The strategy might consist of individual contacts, telephone recruiting using community phone books that contain family members and ages of children, and referrals from knowledgeable residents in the community.

One of the positive features of volunteer assistance in recruiting is that these individuals might be able to use existing community contacts and networks in the recruitment effort. Furthermore, the volunteers are likely to be familiar with the demands and pressure on the prospective participants and may be able to identify persuasive and innovative recruitment strategies.

Nonresearchers can also serve as focus group moderators. In some situations, volunteers may actually be preferable for moderating focus groups, as in situations when limited resources do not allow for professional moderators or some staff members of the organization have limited skills in group interaction or high visibility.

In some communities, the staff members of the nonprofit organization are well known and at times seen as the embodiment of the agency. These staff members may be seen as instructors, administrators, or advocates of valued social issues, and, consequently, their role within the agency impedes their ability to moderate focus groups. For example, a county agricultural agent who has repeatedly advocated improved farming methods may want to know reasons why these methods are not being adopted. Farmers in focus groups will likely be selective in responding to the inquiries of the agent moderator and may avoid sharing insights that reflect badly on the agent. For similar reasons, I have discouraged the use of volunteer moderators who are readily identified with community issues.

The moderating function is one of the critical components of a focus group and, to a large extent, the quality of the results are directly related to the skills of the moderator. It has been my experience that careful screening plus approximately 12 hours of training have been adequate to prepare moderators for conducting focus group discussions. In these cases, the moderators did not develop the questioning route or coordinate the analysis, and additional training would be needed to provide minimal competency in this area.

Moderators must be selected with care. Some people have an affinity for the task and can listen sincerely, ask open-ended questions, and probe even without special training. Because of these innate skills, careful selection of volunteers is well advised and other tasks should be arranged for volunteers not possessing the moderating skills.

The training of moderators should focus on achieving competency in several types of skills, including

—smoothly handling the presession small talk and creating a friendly environment, but not providing details of the discussion;

—skillfully introducing the focus group, providing the ground rules and opening question;

—asking questions without referring to the questioning route and using effective follow-up probes;

—remembering the big picture and preparing mentally; and

—maintaining mental discipline and concentration throughout the interview.

Specifically, they need to think in three dimensions as they observe the discussion:

(1) the present—what is happening at this moment;
(2) the next step—thinking one step ahead of the participants and always having a mental picture of what will occur next; and
(3) the meaning of the information provided by the focus group—Are the topics being discussed addressing the critical areas needed in the study? and How will this information be used?

Often, it is helpful to have a researcher experienced with focus groups serve as assistant moderator at the initial focus group interview and offer constructive suggestions in the postmeeting briefing.

Typed transcripts of focus group interviews are a desirable option where volunteers can provide valuable assistance. The transcripts are not essential for the analysis, but, when available, they speed up the analysis process. Without the transcript, the analyst needs to play back the tapes and then rely on memory and field notes from the moderating team—a process that is more taxing without transcripts. The major disadvantage of transcripts is cost. A skilled typist can often produce a transcript in eight hours; however, in most nonprofit organizations, the secretaries are called upon to handle a multitude of tasks with frequent interruptions. Constant interruptions break the concentration of the typist and prolong the transcript production. Consequently, the desired transcripts are set aside because of the day-to-day demands of the office operation. Volunteers, however, can take on this task providing they have the time, proper equipment, adequate knowledge of the topic, and typing skills.

The ideal volunteer for this task should be able to begin the typing the day following the focus group. Often, the first draft of the transcript will contain sections that must be completed by the moderator. Therefore, it is desirable if the transcript is available to the moderator for review within several days following the interview. At times, portions of the tape may be unintelligible or the typist may be uncertain who is making a comment. For example, if the typist was uncertain who made a particular comment, the moderator might be able to supply this information by reading the manuscript and quickly checking the appropriate section of the tape. I've encouraged typists to use parentheses for all sections of the transcript where there is uncertainty due to lack of tape clarity. The moderator can quickly review those sections for revision, addition, or correction.

The volunteer typist must have proper equipment, which includes a cassette tape player with a tone control and four-inch or larger speakers. The small speakers on some cassette recorders can be tedious to listen to and should be avoided. In some situations, headphones can be extremely helpful to the typist. The typing task is simplified if the cassette player has a variable speed control, which will enable the tape to be played back at a slower than normal speed. In addition, some cassette players have a reverse scan button that will back up the tape slightly with the push of a button. It is preferable to have the manuscripts typed on a word processor to allow for later inclusions of missing data. The word processor also allows for the final transcript to be printed with variations in spacing and type size.

The volunteer typist needs to be familiar with the topic being discussed. The typist needs to have a working knowledge of the vocabulary and specialized terms used in the conversation. Finally, the volunteer should have a typing speed of at least 40 words per minute.

NONRESEARCHERS AND
FOCUS GROUP ANALYSIS

Nonresearchers can play a very important part in the analysis of focus group results; however, successful use of nonresearchers in analysis requires planning and matching the task to the skills and abilities of the individual. If the nonresearchers have had direct experience with the area of investigation and also have had past contact with others using the program, then these individuals may be helpful in interpreting the findings. At times, agency professionals may have had selective exposure to the program being investigated, so the wider range of insights from nonresearchers is essential to understanding how the total program is perceived. In other situations, the findings might yield perceptions that have never been shared with the agency staff, and, while they may be new to the professional, they may be common knowledge to lay volunteers.

The analysis process is best accomplished by an individual familiar with qualitative research methodology. This task could be performed by a nonresearcher who is likely to be an agency staff member knowledgeable in focus group procedures. Nonresearchers are able to serve as validity checkers on interpretations and judgments offered by the analyst. The analyst reviews the evidence (findings) and then offers an interpretation to the nonresearchers. Nonresearchers are asked if the interpretation makes sense and if other interpretations might be offered based on the findings. In some situations, multiple interpretations may be offered, but when this occurs, it may be best to advance a primary interpretation with recommendations and then cite alternative interpretations as possibilities.

NONRESEARCHERS AND VOLUNTEERS REPORTING FOCUS GROUP RESULTS

Nonresearchers and volunteers can be of valuable assistance in sharing the results of a focus group study, both formally and informally. If these individuals are asked to assist in this process, it is desirable that they have had reasonable exposure to the focus group process such as in the task force, in moderating, or in analysis of results.

Nicollet County: An Example of Volunteers and Professionals Working Together

Nicollet County is located in southcentral Minnesota, a little over an hour's drive from Minneapolis. Agriculture has traditionally been an important part of the local economy, but in recent years, farming has fallen on hard times. In the past decade, an increasing number of residents have taken off-farm jobs with dual-earner families becoming commonplace. In the midst of these changes, the county extension agents and the local advisory board—the county extension committee— were considering how the county extension service could better serve the needs of residents. Both the extension professionals and the advisory board felt that they needed a reading of how the local residents perceived the agency. After consultation with experts at the University of Minnesota, they agreed to conduct a series of focus groups with target audiences.

The logistical leadership for the study was provided by a county extension agent, but the heart of the study depended on a small core of volunteer moderators identified cooperatively by the professionals and the lay advisory committee. The volunteers received approximately 12 hours of training in focus group procedures and then each volunteer conducted two focus groups in the community. The analysis was performed by university faculty in cooperation with a market research firm. The volunteers provided helpful advice on interpretations and recommendations for future action.

THE USE OF NONRESEARCHERS

Nonresearchers can provide valuable assistance in a focus group project by providing insights, labor, and credibility. The final study may be improved considerably through the use of volunteers and non-researchers, but agency researchers must oversee the process carefully. When volunteers are used, they are members of a team composed of staff members and volunteers, each of whom possesses talents and perceptions. The professional researchers must believe in the wisdom of nonresearchers. This cooperative effort can draw out the best of both professionals and nonresearchers if it is planned carefully and if the procedures are skillfully managed.

SUMMARY

Nonresearchers can take on difficult tasks and, with training and supervision, perform these responsibilities in a capable manner. The primary advantage of using nonresearchers or volunteers in focus groups is not simply the cost savings, for if the costs of supervisory time and training are factored, it may be less expensive to hire trained help. Instead, the greatest values are the development of new skills among volunteers—skills that they can transfer to other community problems; increased validity due to volunteers neutrality and insight into interpretations; and enhanced understanding of the needs and challenges of the agency, which can result in better informed supporters.

10

Focus Groups:
Special Situations

The (focus group) technique is robust, hardy, and can be twisted a bit and still yield useful and significant results. This is not an argument for laxity in group design, nor is it an apology for inadequate moderators. Rather, the point here is that flexibility rather than rigor ought to characterize the use of focus groups. (Gerald Linda, 1982, p. 98)

For the casual observer, focus groups seem quite simple. They look like groups of people talking about a common topic of interest, a procedure that seems almost too simple to be called research. Successful focus groups are supposed to look easy. They are similar to the seemingly effortless grace of a master gymnast or the comfortable, relaxed stride of an Olympic marathon runner. They look easy because the moderator has command of the fundamentals and executes the basic principles with comfortable precision. This aura of simplicity has resulted in abuses in qualitative research in general and focus groups in particular. An abuse that occurs with frequency is the mislabeling of focus groups. In some areas of study, *focus groups* has become the "in" term, and quite a variety of group experiences have been misplaced under this rubric. This book has emphasized a somewhat rigorous approach to focus groups, in large part because of the misuses that have occurred in private market research firms, educational organizations, and nonprofit agencies.

Flexibility in the use of focus groups and modification of the procedures can be extremely beneficial if these changes are deliberate and factored into the analysis of the results. Modifications that have merit in certain situations include periodic focus groups repeated with the same participants, focus groups within existing groups of people, focus groups within an organization, focus groups with young people, and telephone focus groups.

PERIODICALLY REPEATED
FOCUS GROUPS

A periodically repeated focus group consists of two or more focus groups on the same topic over a period of time. For example, a community center might conduct annual or even quarterly focus groups with those using the facilities, or a state park system might conduct weekly focus groups with campers. In each of these situations, the organization is able to keep abreast of user perceptions and take corrective action as needed. Bernard Gordon, a consultant from Glencoe, Illinois, suggests:

> Every association needs to audit what it's doing from the perspective of members. Like any other form of evaluation, focus groups should be held on a fairly regular schedule, so that you can begin to compare results. (Lydecker, 1986, p. 74)

Nonprofit organizations, like private sector businesses, find that their services, clientele, and objectives change over time. Original purposes of the organization are modified and adapted by forces in the environment and these changes directly affect members or consumers. Periodic assessment of the organization via focus groups might be performed at several levels. The assessment might concentrate on overall organizational strategy or zero in on specific features of particular interest such as new member recruiting.

Repeated focus groups can also be conducted with the same participants with a time interval between sessions. This use of focus groups is helpful in situations in which the researcher wants to track changes in perceptions over time. Another variation of repeated focus groups is to observe participants who are purposefully brought together with divergent points of view. Martin Buncher (1982, p. 15) refers to these as "presensitized groups." Buncher comments:

> Presensitized groups [are those] where respondents already have participated in one group on the subject and then are brought back for a second group after having learned what the nature of the problem area was, the purpose of the research involved. etc.

> These "enlightened" participants may be asked to interact with advocates of opposing views in a joint session or to reevaluate their opinions as a result of feedback from the first groups.

In these presensitized groups, a degree of moderator skill is required to set the stage for openness and interaction. Participants will likely need reminders that the intent is not to debate the different sides of the issue, but rather to explore each point of view in greater depth. It can be illuminating to discover the logic and rationale used by each side as they present their point of view as they seek to win "converts." If the purpose of the study is to determine persuasive arguments that are convincing to those with differing points of view, then the repeated focus groups with presensitized groups are a sound choice.

SPECIAL FOCUS GROUP STRUCTURES

The structure of the focus group can be modified to accommodate two moderators—either in a dueling or in a complementary role. In the dueling mode, the moderators take planned, predetermined sides and the participants may be either assigned to or choose the side on which they will participate. The primary advantage of the dueling structure is that it "legitimizes" different points of view and "invites" supporting arguments or points of view from the participants. In effect, this structure helps the researchers gain an understanding of how participants construct arguments in order to be most convincing to the opposing side.

Complementary moderators work together but represent different levels of expertise with focus groups and the topic of discussion. For example, one moderator may be an expert in focus groups and a generalist, whereas the second moderator might know little about focus groups but be a specialist in the topic under discussion. In effect, this procedure allows for a subject matter expert in the focus groups, but not in a manner that will unduly influence the group. Suppose that a community center wants to build a new recreational unit and decides to conduct a series of focus groups with members of the community. The moderator with expertise in focus groups might be complemented by a moderator with an architectural background who could present background information on various alternative ideas suggested by the participants. Jeff Pope (1977, p. 150) describes how the procedure is used:

> This approach is especially useful on highly technical subjects where it's virtually impossible to give an outside moderator all the detailed background information he might need. We've had good results in these cases using two moderators: Our own moderator, plus a second moderator from the client. The client moderator is often an R & D expert or someone else familiar with the technical details of the product.

Our moderator is responsible for the flow of the session and the basic probing, while the "expert" moderator follows up on technical issues that might otherwise be overlooked.

A variation of the use of complementary moderators is to have the sponsor of the focus group serve as the second moderator. This might include the director of the nonprofit agency or a member of the board of directors. These situations require some degree of caution as these individuals tend to be rather defensive and to overreact when they hear negative comments. Furthermore, if this second moderator is an individual with local prominence or in a respected position, the participants might have some inhibitions about providing candid feedback.

FOCUS GROUPS WITH EXISTING
GROUPS AND ORGANIZATIONS

While the focus group process is robust, there are several situations where additional caution is needed. One of the areas requiring caution is in using the procedure with existing groups, and especially work groups within an organization. In these environments, the participants are very likely to know each other and possibly work closely. The greatest danger of focus groups in these environments is in the analysis of the results, not in the discussion process. Generally, the discussion process in focus groups is pleasant and enjoyable to participants, and usually people are quite willing to share their ideas and opinions with others. This tendency also holds true when people work together. The problem is in analysis of what was shared. Were participants holding back because of others in the group? Were they being selective in what they said because of others in the group? Were they taking positions on issues simply because of certain other individuals in the group? The analyst cannot know all the dynamics that might have influenced the participants in the discussion.

In spite of these dangers, focus groups can be effectively used in existing organizations and even in work groups. Mitchell Elrod (1981) has used focus groups within organizations to study employee relations, benefits, training, supervision, current or planned marketing programs, quality control measures, and work schedules. In order to obtain this information, Elrod encourages random selection of employees at the same level in the organization to participate in a focus group during business hours, held outside of the office or business in a neutral location. In addition, the focus group is conducted by a professional moderator not affiliated with the organization. Elrod (1981, p. 37) and his colleagues have been pleased with the results of these groups:

To date, the moderators from our firm have had no known problem establishing an atmosphere of mutual confidence with employee groups. In fact, the overwhelming reaction has been one of gratification that "someone up there really does care what I think."

Focus group discussions with exceptional employees (or volunteers) can yield valuable information for organizational decision makers. A series of focus groups with exceptional staff members may produce clues that will maintain their levels of productivity, uncover their secrets of success, or provide suggestions on how the organization can improve. George Zanes, a New Jersey consultant, has found that focus groups produce valuable insights when conducted with key employees. Zanes relates:

We have uncovered those hidden thoughts and attitudes that often get in the way of a person's effective performance, attitudes that the individuals themselves are frequently not aware of as hampering their productivity. ("Focus-Group Techniques," 1985, p. 41)

Focus groups can be effectively used in organizations to provide information about consumers. In most organizations, there are certain individuals who have regular contact with consumers. Focus groups with these frontline staff can provide valuable insights into customer behavior and preferences. For example, a manufacturer will have representatives, salespeople, or repair staff who have insights into customer preferences, problems, and concerns. This information can be of enormous value to the company, but unfortunately it is not solicited. In these situations, Eugene Fram (1985) of the Rochester Institute of Technology recommends the use of in-house focus groups with specialized employees. Fram has conducted focus groups with a variety of frontline employees, such as dealers, manufactures' representatives, maintenance/repair personnel, installation personnel, and secretaries.

In-house focus groups are more productive if attention is placed on achieving a nonthreatening, permissive environment. Extra consideration must be given to explaining the purpose of the discussion to defuse potential sensitivity. In addition, it is important to remind participants that the focus group is part of a research study and not a decision or planning committee. Moderators should avoid creating the impression that the organization will change following the group discussion. Participants are reminded that the intent is to gather information from a number of employees and then share these aggregated perceptions with those who will be making decisions.

The choice of moderator should be given consideration. Moderators from outside of the agency have the advantage of being neutral, but they may be unfamiliar with the organizational culture. Internal moderators are more likely to be familiar with the organization, but they will have the challenge of engendering the confidence and trust of the participants. Participants should be grouped with care. Participants should be placed with others at the same level or status in the organization. Perceptions are most important, but job titles or salary level should also be considered. Perhaps the easiest method to ensure that participants are similar in level is to assemble a list of potential employee participants and then seek feedback from several people about the list.

FOCUS GROUP INTERVIEWS WITH
YOUNG PEOPLE

Focus groups have considerable potential for discovering how young people think about issues, programs, and opportunities; however, special logistic procedures and moderator skills may be essential. When considering focus groups with young people, the researcher should begin by observing them in informal settings. A number of the mistakes that occur when doing focus groups with teens are due to assumptions that they have similar preferences and habits to those of adults. The researcher should consider the following: In what situations do the young people naturally talk and share thoughts with each other? Are adults present when kids talk? If adults are present, how do these adults relate to the youth? How large are the groups? In my observations of teens, I have found that discussions take place on the floor, around a table eating pizza, on the front steps of the school, on the beach, or on the street. Teen focus groups may work better if conducted outside of institutions run by adults where adults make and enforce rules—churches, schools, and even recreation centers.

Focus groups with young people may need to be limited to 60 minutes or less. Young people repeatedly find themselves in environments where change or relocation takes place every 45 to 60 minutes. If the researcher has planned a two-hour focus group discussion, it is likely that there will be a bunch of bored kids for the second hour. Therefore, researchers should limit the questions and, if possible, incorporate things to touch, do, or respond to. For example, a brief one-page survey early or midway through the discussion can be helpful in focusing their attention on future areas of conversation.

The nature of the focus group questions may need some special thought when working with young people. Dichotomous questions that can be answered with a "yes" or "no" should be especially avoided with this group. Adults may assume that the moderator really wants elaboration of the answer but young people often take the question more literally and give one-word answers. Moderators should avoid questions that threaten the independence and freedom of young people. For example, suppose the moderator wanted to know how decisions were made about which high school courses to enroll in. In this situation, the moderator should avoid asking who makes the decision, for few teens want to admit in front of their peers that their parents influence the decision. Instead, it may be more productive to ask teens to think back to the last time the decision was made and describe what happened.

The ideal teen focus group will likely be shorter, smaller, less formal, segregated by sex, and have a moderator with experience in working with kids. Some adults have a knack for getting kids to talk, probably because they exude trust, respect, tolerance, humor, and a willingness to listen. Select a moderator with these positive qualities of interaction.

FOCUS GROUP DISCUSSIONS
ON THE TELEPHONE

Focus group discussions can be conducted on the telephone—a procedure that offers some advantages in assembling people who are difficult to reach. With a conference-call telephone hookup, the moderator can carry on a focus group discussion with people scattered around the country. The telephone focus group offers the advantage of allowing participants to interact over distances at a fraction of the cost of transporting the same people to a central location.

The principle disadvantage of telephone focus groups is the lack of nonverbal communication. Much is gained in focus groups by watching the participants—head nodding, boredom, smiles, frowns, alertness, interest in the topic—all of which are unavailable on the telephone. In this sense, the telephone focus group is one step above the individual telephone interview, but it will lack the richness of evidence characteristic of in-person focus groups.

A telephone focus group can be conducted with varying levels of sophistication. At one extreme, it can be conducted with limited resources and resemble a conference phone call. With more sophisticated telephone equipment, it is possible to have a console with lights and name tags to identify speakers, special switching devices that allow only one person to speak at a time, and lights that indicate when others are attempting to talk.

ISSUES WHEN ADAPTING
FOCUS GROUPS

When adapting focus groups to other types of situations, the researcher should bear in mind what the focus group can do and what it can't do. While there is elasticity in the procedure, too much stretch may rupture the process. When adapting focus groups, consideration should be given to

(1) The purpose of the effort. It is appropriate to use focus groups to collect information, to listen, and to learn. It is not appropriate to use focus groups if the intent is to teach, to inform, to tell, or have others sanction a decision.

(2) The people involved in the process. Focus groups participants are preselected. Open invitations to the public or blanket invitations to a group are not used in focus group interviews.

(3) The nature of the discussion. A focused interview comprises primarily open-ended questions that allow participants to select the manner of their response. It is not an open discussion of anything of interest.

(4) The nature of the environment. The focused interview is conducted in a permissive environment conducive to sharing, listening, and responding. It is not a place where judgments are made about the quality or worth of other comments or where decisions are to be made.

SUMMARY

Focus group interviews have been successfully used in a variety of situations. They can be conducted with the same people over a period of time, on the telephone, with multiple moderators, or with preestablished groups or organizations. All of these adaptations of focus group interviews possess the characteristics of focus groups discussed in Chapter 2. A limited number of homogeneous people are invited to participate in a focused discussion in order to provide data of a qualitative nature. The purpose is not to teach, to provide therapy, to resolve differences, or to achieve a consensus, but to obtain information in a systematic and verifiable manner. With that purpose in mind, the researcher should be encouraged to "twist it a bit" and discover just how robust and hardy focus group interviews really are.

11

Contracting for Focus Groups: A Consumer's Guide

Focus groups do not have to be designed and conducted by an agency. Rather, consultants can provide such services for a fee. How does one contract for such services? Here are some suggestions.

IDENTIFICATION OF A RESEARCH FIRM

The first step is to identify the potential research firms or individuals in the community who conduct focus group interviews. Marketing or advertising people in larger companies can offer advice about names of people and market research firms. Larger companies may subcontract some of their market research to local individuals and firms, and their recommendations may prove quite helpful. Another approach is to identify knowledgeable individuals and seek their advice. For example, professors in schools of business or local evaluators may provide helpful leads. In addition, the membership directories of professional organizations such as the American Evaluation Association or the American Marketing Association list potential consultants.

INITIAL CONTACT WITH POTENTIAL CONTRACTORS

Telephone calls to potential consultants will help reduce the list to manageable proportions. When making initial contacts, the following information is useful:

What experience have they had with focus groups?

Do they specialize in certain product areas?

How large is their research staff?

How long have they been in business?

Will they provide a list of past clients?

Are they willing to prepare a formal proposal, describing their procedures, time line, and costs?

This initial telephone visit should assist in narrowing the field to those consultants who seem interested and have the requisite experience. It is often best to solicit proposals from two or three of the most promising. If time permits, it is often helpful to go to the office of the consultant for further discussions because examples of past work are in vendor files. Often, one can view the discussion room or, in general, size up the operation.

MAKING THE DECISION

In making the decision about contracting, cost alone is not the key factor; however, it should be considered. Consultants with past experience, a successful track record, and satisfied clients are preferred. The prospective client should give thought to the degree to which the research firm or individual consultant understands his or her specific problems or issues. This is accomplished by talking to the moderator who will be conducting the interviews and considering rapport with this individual.

The head of the research firm or the person representing the firm will not necessarily serve as moderator. The client should ask who would be doing the moderating and also request to speak to that person. The moderator should convey interest and enthusiasm for the project, while also demonstrating an ability to listen and be empathic. The client should be comfortable with the moderator's communication skills—both oral and written.

The moderator's role in the analysis is an area of special concern. The potential moderator should be asked to comment on the number of groups that would be involved and the analysis process. The moderator might be asked to explain the sequence of steps involved in the analysis. One of the best ways to assess the potential of the prospective consultant is to look over focus group reports. Some reports are proprietary and cannot be shared, but if no reports are available for inspection, it may be a signal that few have been completed. When reviewing these focus group reports, the client should identify the reporting style preferred (raw data, descriptive summary, or interpretative) for the study being considered. Several options might be available in terms of the final report. A number of consultants limit themselves to preparing reports that only highlight participant comments. By scanning through other reports prepared by the moderator, the client can tell if the analysis goes beyond what was said and includes what the participants meant.

In a number of situations, the client will need only specialized assistance from the consultant. For example, preexisting groups or address lists may reduce the costs of participant recruitment. Oral-only reports, written mini-reports, and comprehensive written reports will each have differing costs. The client might want to consider the option of focus group training for agency employees. This training could be in a classroom style or experiential, where selected employees work alongside an experienced moderator as an apprentices. The benefit of training is that the agency gains not only a report but trained employees who can replicate the experiences as needed.

HOW MUCH SHOULD IT COST?

The costs for focus group interviews can vary considerably depending on a number of factors such as location, type of audience, selection process for participants, and number of groups. Here's a lower cost estimate that may prove helpful. Assume that four focus groups are to be held locally involving people randomly selected from telephone interviews. Here is how the costs might break down:

Planning 8 hrs @ $50 per hr	$ 400.
Phone recruiting @ 60 hrs $10 per hr	$ 600.
Gifts to participants 48 @ $20 each	$ 960.
Meal & room 48 @ $15 each	$ 720.
Moderator expense 20 hrs @ $50 per hr	$1000.
Analysis & report prep 40 hrs @ $50 per hr	$2000.
Moderator's travel	$ 100.
Typing transcripts 40 hrs @ $10 per hour	$ 400.
Typing report 16 hrs @ $10 per hr	$ 160.
Paper, supplies, & overhead	$ 300.
Oral report 4 hrs @ $50 per hr	$ 200.

Total $6840.

Thus in a relatively small focus group contract, it would not be surprising to find estimates in the neighborhood of $7000. Remember that this example is only to illustrate the pricing considerations in developing a cost estimate for a series of focus group interviews. The costs of focus group projects can and do vary considerably and can range from nothing (where all time and expenses are included in other budgets) to $1000 where selected moderator services are purchased to $7000 or more for contracting out the entire project. Typically, the budget estimates provided by consultants will not break down individual parts of the process, but they might provide cost estimates for various options in reporting or recruiting.

CONTRACTING FOR SPECIAL NEEDS

At times, the client will have focus group needs that necessitate a special contract, such as designing the study, staff training, moderating, diagnostic feedback to moderators, or audits of the draft or final reports.

(1) Contract for designing the focus group study. Much of the success depends on how well the focus group study is planned and designed. An outside expert might plan the details of a focus group study using staff and resources internal to the contracting organization. For example, the expert might be under contract for several days to obtain background information on the purposes of the study, to develop the questioning route, to identify the sampling strategy, to prepare the telephone screening survey, to train a small core of moderators, and to outline a master plan for implementing the study.

(2) Contract for diagnostic feedback to moderators. Focus groups are typically conducted over a time span of several weeks and consist of a number of different discussion groups. It is often valuable to receive diagnostic feedback early in the series of focus groups to identify strengths of the moderator and areas needing improvement for future focus groups. Without this feedback, moderators tend to repeat unproductive moderating activities and thereby limit the amount and quality of participant discussion. The procedure calls for listening to the focus group tape (while reviewing the transcript, if available) and examination of the field notes and analysis report prepared by the moderating team. Using this information, the reviewer prepares a written assessment of the moderator and the focus group process.

The feedback report consists of two parts. The first section addresses the skills and capabilities of the moderator, with helpful feedback to the moderator. Included are a written assessment of the strengths and weaknesses of the moderator, with suggestions for improvement as needed. The second section of the feedback report concentrates on the analysis summary prepared by the moderator. Specific attention is placed on matching the interpretation to the evidence contained in the tape or transcript. If appropriate, additional suggestions of "big ideas" are provided.

(3) Contract for an outside audit of the focus group report. A written report is prepared at the conclusion of the series of focus group interviews. The outside audit consists of an outside expert reviewing the draft report and suggesting changes as needed prior to publishing the final focus group report. Experts review all available raw materials from the series of focus groups, including tapes, transcripts, field notes, analysis reports prepared by moderators of individual focus groups, and a double-spaced draft of the final report. After reviewing the raw materials, the consultant makes notations and suggestions directly on the draft report with an indication of the level of importance of each of the suggested changes. When changes are needed, the expert does not draft the revision, but rather provides an outline of what might be included. This draft with suggestions is then returned for future revisions, as needed. The expert auditor also prepares a cover letter, which can be inserted in the report. This letter provides an official judgment about the quality of the analysis process.

SUMMARY

The decision to contract for outside help in conducting focus groups is typically motivated by several factors: the desire to maintain quality control in the process, the lack of internal staff to conduct the study, or the need for a neutral party to conduct the study. Of these factors, the most difficult to monitor is quality control, because cost alone is not the indicator of quality. To be sure, experts who are experienced with focus group procedures can often provide the elements that result in quality: an appropriate sampling strategy, a well-developed questioning route, skillful moderating, and systematic analysis. Some of the most beneficial focus group studies, however, have been conducted by internal staff members with very limited budgets.

Postscript:
The Future of Focus Groups

Individuals and organizations within the public and private non-profit sector have found focus group interviewing to be helpful. Indeed, the term *helpful* may be an understatement, for a sizable number of individuals have found that this procedure provides insights and information of considerable benefit. For a number of years I have had the good fortune to provide methodological advice on evaluation and research studies. During this time, I have encouraged seekers of information to use a variety of methods, including mail-out and telephone surveys, individual interview, tests, and observations. The selection and mix of procedures was driven by the nature of the information needs and the capabilities of the researcher. Focus group interviewing stands apart from other methodological procedures in one interesting respect. When the study was completed the researchers (and the decision makers) regularly got excited about both the process and the results. Occasionally, a researcher might get excited about a mail-out survey or a series of individual interviews, but more often these processes were tedious work necessary to fulfill some information needs. By contrast, research veterans of focus group interviewing displayed sincere enthusiasm for the benefits of the process. In part, it was this user enthusiasm that prompted my efforts in preparing this book.

Focus group interviewing is beneficial to nonprofit organizations in two respects. First, the procedure introduces a systematic and organized means of listening to people. Organizations regularly suffer from limitations on feedback. The focus group interview introduces a process of listening, and this process conveys positive impressions of the organization. In exit comments at the conclusion of focus groups, participants are regularly upbeat; for example:

I enjoyed the chance to talk about this topic.

I'm impressed that the organization is listening to our views.

They must think that we are important because they really made an effort to listen.

I feel honored that you listened to me.

Thank you for coming out to listen.

This organized process of listening conveys positive impressions that the organization really cares about, and is concerned with, the views of clients, employees, volunteers, or residents of the community.

The second organizational benefit of focus groups is in the nature of the information obtained. Focus groups yield insights about the organization, the programs, and the environment that have been of substantial assistance to decision makers. For example, in the study of vocational technical education (Peterson & Migler, 1986), earlier recommendations derived from other survey methods did not translate into the desired result—increased participation. By contrast, when the recommendations of the focus groups were applied the result was a tenfold enrollment boost. The earlier procedure, while carefully executed, simply did not provide information on the critical factors affecting increased enrollment.

The Educational Media Services Department of the Minneapolis Public Schools recently conducted a series of focus groups with media specialists on a proposed new curriculum. At the conclusion of the study, Gladys Sheehan, director of the department and the person who commissioned the study, commented:

> The focus group process is especially useful for decision makers in public organizations. The study we recently conducted will be useful to our education team as we develop future directions for the media curriculum. The process was helpful to us because it permitted maximum participant input, controlled the attention of the group to the topic under consideration, and was an effective tool for uncovering layers of information and attitudes from individuals. The net result was decisions and programs that reflect the collective wisdom of the group. (G. Sheehan, personal communication, March 14, 1988)

This book is intended to assist researchers by improving their skills and abilities in planning, conducting, analyzing, and reporting results of focus group interviews. Careful, systematic listening is of value all by itself, but when combined with the suggestions incorporated in this book, the listening can achieve increased focus, greater depth, and more insights, and consequently can provide a finished product valued by the organization.

The future of focus groups will depend upon a sound recognition of the limits of the procedure. Focus groups can be a refreshing and appealing means of obtaining information. On the other hand, focus groups have some seductive qualities that tempt researchers and decision makers to use them in unwarranted situations. They are seductive in several ways: The results are understandable, the participants typically enjoy the opportunity to participate, and the process creates a favorable impression that the sponsoring organization really cares enough to listen to people. Indeed, these are major advantages, but they can also tempt users to misuse and abuse the technique.

Focus groups provide a special type of information. They provide a richness of data at a reasonable cost. They tap into the real-life interactions of people and allow the researcher to get in touch with participants' perceptions, attitudes, and opinions in a way that other procedures do not allow. Decision makers have needed this type of information in the past, they need it now, and, because of increased pressure for accountability, they will need it even more in the future.

References

Readers wishing further information on focus groups, but with limited time, may wish to consult the starred (*) references.

*Advertising Research Foundation. (1985). *Focus groups: Issues and approaches.* New York: Author.

Alkin, Marvin C., Daillak, Richard, & White, Peter. (1979). *Using evaluations.* Beverly Hills, CA: Sage.

Anderson, Leith. (1986). Is Baptist important in our church's name? *The Standard, 76*(5), 25, 27, 29.

Andreasen, Alan R. (1983). Cost-conscious marketing research. *Harvard Business Review, 83*(4), 74-79.

Andrews, Amy. (1977, July 11). How to buy productive focus group research. *Advertising Age,* pp. 128, 147, 148.

Antilla, Susan, & Sender, Henriette. (1982). Getting consumers in focus. *Dun's Business Month, 119*(5), 78-80.

Applied Management Sciences, Inc. (1977). *An assessment of parent education and general needs that can be served by educational programming for television. Executive summary G-98.* Silver Spring, MD: Author. (ERIC Document Reproduction Service No. ED 143 361)

Arfken, Deborah E. (1985, April). *Running at double pace: Women in dual-profession marriages.* Paper presented at the 69th Annual Conference of the National Association for Women Deans, Administrators, and Counselors, Milwaukee, WI. (ERIC Document Reproduction Service No. ED 260 343)

A step-by-step way to conduct worthwhile focus groups. (1978). *Training, 15*(12), 50, 55.

Axelrod, Myril D. (1975a, February 28). Marketers get an eyeful when focus groups expose products, ideas, images, ad copy, etc. to consumers. *Marketing News,* pp. 6-7.

Axelrod, Myril D. (1975b, March 14). 10 Essentials for good qualitative research. *Marketing News,* pp. 5-8.

Axelrod, Myril D. (1984, June 8). Qualitative research: An underdeveloped direct marketing aid. *Marketing News,* pp. 6, 7.

Bailey, Douglas M. (1984). A herd of elephants pitches floppy disk for Dennison Mfg. *New England Business, 6*(20), 40, 42.

Baker, Philip N. (1985). Focus group interviewing: The real constituency. *Journal of Data Collection, 25*(2), 14-23.

Barnes, Win. (1978). What testing has taught Shell about its mail order customers. *Direct Marketing, 41*(5), 61-72.

Bartos, Rena. (1986). Qualitative research: What it is and where it came from. *Journal of Advertising Research, 26*(3), RC3-RC6.

Basch, Charles E. (1987). Focus group interview: An underutilized research technique for improving theory and practice in health education. *Health Education Quarterly, 14*(4), 411-448.

Beck, Leif C., Trombetta, W. L., & Share, S. (1986). Using focus group sessions before decisions are made. *North Carolina Medical Journal, 47*(2), 73-74.

Becker, Sandra. (1986). *Focus group report on the Institute for Technical Communications.* Unpublished paper, University of Minnesota, Department of Rhetoric, St. Paul.

*Beckett, Kathleen. (1985). Focus groups: A market research tool. *Credit Union Executive, 25*(1), 8-12, 15.

Bellenger, Danny N., Bernhardt, Kenneth L., & Goldstrucker, Jac L. (1976). Qualitative research techniques: Focus group interviews. In *Qualitative Research in Marketing.* Chicago: American Marketing Association. (Reprinted in James B. Higginbotham, & Keith K. Cox, Eds., 1979. *Focus group interviews: A reader.* Chicago: American Marketing Association)

Bengston, Roger E. (1980, September 19). Despite controversy, focus groups are used to examine wide range of marketing questions. *Marketing News*, pp. 18, 25.

Bengston, Roger E. (1982, May 14). A powerful qualitative marketing research tool, One-on-one depth interviewing has 7 advantages. *Marketing News*, p. 21.

Bennett, Amanda. (1986, June 3). Once a tool of market researchers, focus groups gain wider usage. *The Wall Street Journal*, p. 1.

Berdine, Rudy. (1986, July 18). Why some students fail to participate in class. *Marketing News*, pp. 23-24.

Bernstein, Donald. (1978, July 10). Focus group rapport can mislead. *Advertising Age, 49*(28), 50, 55.

Berry, Leonard L., Zeithaml, Valerie A., & Parasuraman, A. (1985). Quality counts in services, too. *Business Horizons, 28*(3), 44-52.

Berryman-Fink, Cynthia, & Fink, Charles B. (1985). Optimal training for opposite-sex managers. *Training & Development Journal, 39*(2), 26-29.

Bers, Trudy H. (1986). Exploring institutional images through focus group interviews. *New Directions for Institutional Research, No. 54 (Designing and Using Marketing Research), 14*(2), 19-29.

Bertrand, Kate. (1986). Listening to the market before speaking up. *Business Marketing, 71*(2), 50-61.

Betts, Nancy M. (1985). A method to measure perceptions of food among the elderly. *Journal of Nutrition for the Elderly, 4*(4), 15-21.

Beveridge, William Ian Beadmore. (1950). *The art of scientific investigation.* Melbourne: Heinemann.

Beyond psychographics: How much you like yourself is the key. (1984). *Ad Forum, 5*(11), 16, 18.

The big difference in K-Mart apparel. (1986). *Discount Merchandiser, 26*(8), 86-104.

Blosser, Betsy J. et al. (1985, May). *The highway safety mass media youth project: A media campaign aimed at drunk driving and seat belt use.* Paper presented at the annual meeting of the International Communication Association, Honolulu, HI.

Bobrow, Edwin E. (1985). Small companies can test, too. *Sales & Marketing Management, 134*(4), 107-110.

Bogart, Beth. (1986, February 13). Test marketing: Politicians campaign for pretested ads. *Advertising Age*, pp. 20-21, 24.

Bookbinder, Stephen M. (1984). Measuring and managing corporate culture. *Human Resource Planning, 7*(1), 47-53.

Bortree, William H. (1986). Focus groups reduce innovation risks. *Bank Marketing, 18*(11), 18-24.

Bourgeois, Jacques C., & Helm, Barbara. (1985). Parenting and communication: A qualitative analysis key to marketing parenting services. *Health Marketing Quarterly, 2*(4), 131-143.

Brewster, Larry. (1984). One step market analysis. *Marketing & Media Decisions, 19*(4), 94-98.

Brinkerhoff, Robert O. et. al. (1983). *Program Evaluation.* Boston: Kluwer-Nijhoff.

Brown, Eric S., & Baumgartner, Robert M. (1985). Financial assistance programs for low-income utility customers. *Public Utilities Fortnightly, 116*(13), 22-28.

Brown, James N. (1986). Purchasing solutions come in a unique package from Xerox. *Purchasing World, 30*(6), 61-63.

Brown, Judy. (1981). How a community bank kept its ear to the ground. *Bank Marketing, 13*(9), 23-26.

Buggie, Frederick D. (1983). Focus on a good idea. *Marketing (UK), 13*(7), 33-40.

Buncher, Martin M. (1982a, September 17). Focus groups seem easy to do and use, but they're easier to misuse and abuse. *Marketing News,* pp. 14-15.

Buncher, Martin M. (1982b, September 17). Six focus group cases: 3 correct, 3 incorrect applications. *Marketing News,* p. 15.

Burnett, John J. (1981). Psychographic and demographic characteristics of blood donors. *Journal of Consumer Research, 8*(1), 62-66.

Bussewitz, Walter. (1986). Private pensions: Where are they going? (Part 2). *Life Association News, 81*(8), 25-31.

Byrne, Andrew J. (1984a). Focus groups: Valuable data, but not basis of sales forecasts. *Direct Marketing, 46*(11), 66-72.

Byrne, Andrew J. (1984b). Some pro's 'n con's about focus groups. *National Underwriter (Life/Health), 88*(29), 3, 18-19, 24-25.

*Calder, Bobby J. (1977). Focus groups and the nature of qualitative marketing research. *Journal of Marketing Research, 14*(3), 353-364.

Calder, Bobby J. (1978, October 20). Surveys' objective: To improve focus group studies. *Marketing News,* pp. 1, 5.

Campbell, Jean P. (1988, January 4). Ease anxieties of elderly or disabled participants during focus groups. *Marketing News,* pp. 1-2.

Caruso, Thomas E. (1976, September 10). Moderators focus on groups: Session yields 7 hypotheses covering technology trend, professionalism, training, techniques, reports, etc. *Marketing News,* pp. 12-16.

Casey, Mary A., Leske, Gary, & Krueger, Richard A. (1987, February). *Marketing agricultural education.* Paper presented at the meeting of the Agricultural Education Central States Research Conference, Chicago.

Cash is not the only virtue. (1986). *Chain Store Age Executive, 62*(10), 78-82.

Chesterton, G. K. (1951). *The Father Brown omnibus: The invisible man.* New York: Dodd, Mead.

Churchill, Gilbert A., Jr. (1983). *Marketing research: Methodological foundation.* Chicago: Dryden.

Client needs dictate focus group report's style, format, content. (1975, October 24). *Marketing News,* pp. 1, 6.

Coe, Barbara J., & MacLachlan, James H. (1980). How major TV advertisers evaluate commercials. *Journal of Advertising Research, 20*(6), 51-54.

Cohen, Barry, & Lippert, Judy. (1985). Building the automated focus group recruiting system. *Journal of Data Collection, 25*(2), 30-33.

Cohen, Ronald Jay. (1985). Computer-enhanced qualitative research. *Journal of Advertising Research, 25*(3), 48-52.

Cohlan, Joan G. (1984). Credit marketing: JC Penney takes a strategic approach. *Credit World, 73*(1), 16-18.

Competition among CUs is like walking on eggs. (1985). *Union Magazine, 51*(3), 8-14.

Constanzo, Gerald L. (1984, August 3). Dollhouse technique focuses on building dreamhouses. *Marketing News*, p. 15.

Consumers talk: Focus group discusses finance company experiences. (1986). *Credit, 12*(4), 10-11.

Cook, Mark. (1970). Experiments on orientation and proxemics. *Human Relations, 23*(1), 61-76.

Cook, Michele. (1986, December 3). Zoo looking for a new lab tag: Maybe it's a pet peeve. *St. Paul Pioneer Press Dispatch*, p. 1D.

Cora, Ellen C. (1986). Use respondent facades to increase focus group productivity. *Medical Marketing & Media, 21*(3), 11-18.

Corporation for Public Broadcasting. (1981). *A comparison of three research methodologies for pilot testing new television programs* (Report no. ISBN-O-89776-0697). Washington, DC: Author. (ERIC Document Reporting Service No. ED 210 712)

Cox, K. K., Higginbotham J. B., & Burton, J. (1976). Applications of focus group interviews in marketing. *Journal of Marketing, 40*(1), 77-80. (Houston, TX: University of Houston, College of Business and Higginbotham Associates)

Danko, William D., & Boucher, David L. (1985). Perspectives from users of obstetric services: Implications for providers. *Health Marketing Quarterly, 3*(1), 41-48.

Das, T. Hari. (1983). Qualitative research in organizational behaviour. *Journal of Management Studies (UK), 20*(3), 301-314.

Davis, Dana. (1985). BASF strives to make plan crystal clear. *Business Insurance, 19*(31), 16-17.

Davis, Junius A. et al. (1986). *Mission, enrollment and staffing patterns, funding procedures, and administration and governance. The North Carolina Community College Study. Executive Summary* (Report no. RTI-3546/00/01ES). Research Triangle Park, NC: Research Triangle Institute. (ERIC Document Reproduction Service No. ED 270 152)

Dellens, Mike. (1979, April). *Math anxiety: What can a learning center do about it?* Paper presented at the annual meeting of the Western College Reading Association. (ERIC Document Reproduction Service No. ED 176 963)

Demby, Emanuel H. (1984, January 6). The marketing researcher: A professional statistician, social scientist—not just another business practitioner. *Marketing News*, pp. 20-21.

DeVogel, Susan H. (1986). Clergy morale: The ups and downs. *The Christian Century, 103*(39), 1149-1152.

Dexter, Lewis Anthony. (1970). *Elite and specialized interviewing.* Evanston, IL: Northwestern University Press.

Diamond, W. D., & Gagnon, J. P. (1985). Obtaining pharmacy class feedback through the use of focus group interviews. *American Journal of Pharmaceutical Education, 49*(1), 49-54.

Dietary concerns, physical limitations are top senior citizen complaints about supermarkets. (1983, February 3). *Marketing News*, p. 8.

Don't operate in the dark. (1985). *Credit Union Magazine, 51*(9), 31-32.

du Pont, George. (1983, May 13). Use telephone to "attend" distant qualitative research sessions. *Marketing News*, p. 19.

Durgee, Jeffery F. (1986). Point of view: Using creative writing techniques in focus groups. *Journal of Advertising Research, 26*(6), 57-65.

Egbert, Harry A. (1983). Focus groups: A basic tool to probe buyers' attitudes. *Industrial Marketing, 68*(3), 82, 84.

Elliott, Peggy G., Ingersoll, Gary M., & Smith, Carl B. (1984). Trends and attitudes in the use of educational media and materials. *Educational Technology, 24*(4), 19-24.

Elrod, J. Mitchell, Jr. (1981). Improving employee relations with focus groups. *Business, 31*(6), 36-38.

Emanuel, Myron. (1984). Industry's middle managers angry and alienated. *Communication World, 13*, 18-19.

Erickson, Julie Liesse. (1986, August 18). JWT gives food for thought for Kraft: Consumer magazine. *Advertising Age*, pp. S2, S4-S5.

Erkut, Sumru & Fields, Jacqueline P. (1987). Focus groups to the rescue. *Training and Development Journal, 4*(10), 74-76.

Feinberg, Andrew. (1984). Inside the entrepreneur. *Venture, 6*(5), 80-86.

Feinberg, Richard A., Snuggs, Thelma L., & Bauer, Sarah B. (1983). The mobility enterprise: An innovative shared transportation system. *Man-Environment Systems, 13*(2), 87-96.

Fern, Edward F. (1982a). The use of focus groups for idea generation: The effects of group size, acquaintanceship, and moderator on response quantity and quality. *Journal of Marketing Research, 19*(1), 1-13.

Fern, Edward F. (1982b). Why do focus groups work: A review and integration of small group process theories. *Advances in Consumer Research, 9*, 444-452.

Fern, Edward F. (1983). Focus groups: A review of some contradictory evidence, implications, and suggestions for future-research. *Advances in Consumer Research, 10*, 121-126.

Festervand, Troy A. (1985). An introduction and application of focus group research to the health care industry. *Health Marketing Quarterly, 2*(2), 199-209.

Fink, Arlene, & Kosecoff, Jacqueline. (Eds.). (1978, April). How to manage an evaluation. *How to Evaluate Education Programs, 2*(4), 1-7. (Washington, DC: Capital Publications)

Finley, Michael. (1987, March). Marketing: Man-on-the-street research yields insights other techniques can't grasp. *Business/Minnesota*, pp. 34-39.

Fitch, Ed. (1984, May 10). Premiums and promotions: Without a plan, the carrots just dangle. *Advertising Age*, pp. M-15-M-17, M-48.

Flegal, David W. (1983). How to control the cost of research. *Madison Avenue, 25*(1), 35-36, 38.

Focus groups are used as bait in trolling for ideas. (1987, August 28). *Marketing News*, p. 48.

Focus group magic may be smothering other research tools. (1975, October 24). *Marketing News*, pp. 1, 7.

Focus group techniques study employee attitudes. (1985, November 8). *Marketing News*, p. 41.

Focus groups aid search for new markets. (1986, January 3). *Marketing News*, p. 54.

Focus groups are a phone call away. (1986, January 3). *Marketing News*, pp. 22, 42.

Focus groups being subverted by clients. (1984, June 8). *Marketing News*, p. 7.

Focus groups, surveys help TV station launch local game show. (1986, October 10). *Marketing News*.

Folch-Lyon, E., de la Macorra, L., & Schearer, S. B. (1981). Focus group and survey research on family planning in Mexico. *Studies in Family Planning, 12*(12), 409-432 (Mexico City: Piata Mexico AC, Shakespeare. Queretaro: Profam. New York: Population Council, Programs Int.)

Folch-Lyon, E., & Trost, J. F. (1981). Conducting focus group sessions. *Studies in Family Planning, 12*(12), 443-449 (Mexico City: Piata Mexico AC, Shakespeare. Norwalk, CT: Trost Associates Inc.)

Fram, Eugene H. (1985). How focus groups unlock market intelligence: Tapping in-house "researchers." *Business Marketing, 70*(12), 80, 82.

Frannin, Rebecca. (1986). Foods: The right stuff. *Marketing & Media Decisions,* [Special Winter issue] *21*(4), 14-18.

Furlong, Carla B., & Ritchie, J. R. Brent. (1986). Consumer concept testing of personal financial services. *International Journal of Bank Marketing (UK), 4*(1), 3-18.

Gage, Theodore J. (1980a, August 25). Ads targeted at mature in need of creative hoist. *Advertising Age*, pp. S-1-S-5.

Gage, Theodore J. (1980b, February 4). Theories differ on use of focus group. *Advertising Age*, pp. S-19, S-20-S-22.

Gantz, Walter. (1980, March). *Uses and gratifications associated with exposure to public television* (Report No. ISBN-0-89776-044-1). Washington, DC: Corporation for Public Broadcasting, Office of Communication Research. (ERIC Document Reproduction Service No. ED 205 162)

Gaylord, Brian S. (1984). Finding out what readers think about Telecom ads. *Telephony, 207*(8), 30-34.

Gelb, Betsy D., & Cheney, Richard J. (1986). Pre-testing jurors' reactions to corporate marketing decisions. *Journal of Public Policy & Marketing, 5*, 97-104.

Gendler, Neal. (1986, July 12). Even churches can use advertising. *Minneapolis Star and Tribune*, p. 17A.

Gives guidelines to set up, use, and analyze focus groups. (1975, October 24). *Marketing News*, pp. 1, 6.

Glaser, Barney G., & Strauss, Anselm L. (1967). *The discovery of grounded theory: Strategies for qualitative research*. Hawthorne, NY: Aldine de Gruyter.

Goldman, Alfred E. (1962, July). The group depth interview. *Journal of Marketing*, pp. 61-68.

*Goldman, Alfred E. & McDonald, Susan Schwartz. (1987). *The group depth interview: Principles and practice*. Englewood Cliffs, NJ: Prentice-Hall.

Goodman, R. Irwin. (1982). Evaluate your media just like the pros. *Instructional Innovator, 27*(7), 27-31.

Goodman, R. Irwin. (1984). Focus group interviews in media product testing. *Educational Technology, 24*(8), 39-44.

Greenberg, Eric Rolfe. (1986). Staying close to the customer. *Management Review, 75*(4), 61-62.

*Greenbaum, Thomas L. (1988). *The practical handbook and guide to focus group research*. Lexington, MA: D.C. Heath.

Grossman, Jack H. (1979, January 12). Qualitative research model can help probe. *Marketing News*, p. 10.

Gutman, Jonathan, & McConaughy, David. (1978). Ambivalence and indifference in preference for television programs. *Journal of Broadcasting, 22*(3), 373-384.

Haddow, David Forbes. (1986). Low-cost real estate consumer analysis can pay off. *Real Estate Review, 16*(2), 85-89.

Haller, Terry P. (1984, May 25). Research method identifies strategic options for firms in mature or declining industries. *Marketing News*, p. 18.

Hammond, Meryl. (1986). Creative focus groups: Uses and misuses. *Marketing & Media Decisions, 21*(8), 154, 156.

Hanna, Maggie. (1979). A perspective in focus groups. In James B. Higginbotham & Keith K. Cox (Eds.), *Focus group interviewing: A reader.* Chicago: American Marketing Association.

*Hansler, Daniel F., & Cooper, Catherine. (1986). Focus groups: New dimension in feasibility study. *Fund Raising Management, 17*(5), 78-82.

Harris, J. Robert, II. (1981, October 16). Focus groups offer six "guidelines" for Black-oriented ads. *Marketing News*, pp. 5, 14.

Heimann-Ratain, Giselle, Hanson, Molly, & Peregay, Stephen M. (1985). The role of focus group interviews in designing a smoking prevention program. *Journal of School Health, 55*(1), 13-16.

Hendricks, Michael. (1984). Preparing and using briefing charts. *Evaluation News, 5*(3), 78-80.

Henkin, Joel. (1979, September 21). Time to stop talking about problems and do something, such as "cold" recruiting. *Marketing News*, p. 4.

Herman, Raymond O. (1982). Focus groups: Bank management beware. *Bank Marketing, 14*(10), 20-32.

Hess, John M. (1971). Group interviewing. In Gerald S. Albaum & M. Venkatesan (Eds.), *Scientific marketing* (pp. 231-233). Glencoe, IL: Free Press.

*Higginbotham, James B., & Cox, Keith K. (Eds.). (1979). *Focus group interviews: A reader.* Chicago: American Marketing Association.

Higgins, Kevin. (1983, October 28). Meticulous planning pays dividends at Stouffer's. *Marketing News*, pp. 1, 20.

Higgins, Kevin. (1984, February 3). Research technique helps students focus on good packaging elements. *Marketing News*, pp. 11, 12.

Hillebrandt, Ina S. (1979). Focus-group research: Behind the one-way mirror. *Public Relations Journal, 35*(2), 17, 33.

Hisrich, R. D., & Peters, M. P. (1982). Focus groups: An innovative marketing-research technique. *Hospital & Health Services Administration, 27*(4), 8-21.

Hitt, Charles, & Cavusgil, S. Tamer. (1985, September 17). Study shows consumers receptive to hospital ads. *Marketing News*, pp. 21-22.

Hogg, David H., & Dunn, Douglas. (1982, June). *Marketing the uniqueness of small towns. Small town strategy* (Report No. WREP-57). Corvallis: Oregon State University, Western Rural Development Center. (ERIC Document Reproduction Service No. ED 227 986)

Holcomb, Betty. (1985). The focus groupie. *Madison Avenue, 27*(9), 47, 50, 57.

Hollander, Sharon L. (1984, January 6). How to control the "alter leader" in qualitative marketing research. *Marketing News*, pp. 18-19.

Hollander, Sharon L., & Oromaner, Daniel S. (1986, January 3). Seminars fill gap in focus-group training. *Marketing News*, p. 1.

Holtzman, Eleanor, & Boudin, Arthur. (1985, May 24). Database includes more of the people less of the time. *Marketing News*, pp. 11, 20.

Horovitz, Bruce. (1983). Market goofs spur marketing sleuths. *Industry Week, 218*(6), 101, 105.

Houlberg, Rick. (1981, August). *The audience experience with television news: A qualitative study.* Paper presented at the annual meeting of the Association for Education in Journalism. (ERIC Document Reproduction Service No. ED 204 756)

How to succeed at small talk. (1987, August). *Glamour,* p. 71.

Howard, Dennis S. (1977, January 28). Don't believe everything you hear in focus groups: Follow these guidelines in evaluating the sessions. *Marketing News,* p. 20.

Huenergard, Celeste. (1977). 153 news columns added by Minneapolis dailies. *Editor & Publisher, 110*(39), 44.

Huey, John. (1985, January 16). What's on a 6-year old's mind? TV shows, TV ads, TV stars. *The Wall Street Journal,* p. 23.

Hutt, Roger W. (1979). The focus group interview: A technique for counseling small business clients. *Journal of Small Business Management, 17*(1), 15-19.

Inflation affects couples' behavior in market place. (1978, May 19). *Marketing News, 11*(23), 8-9.

International Telephone and Telegraph Corp. (1974). *A summary of the research background of the new children's television series* Big Blue Marble (September 1, 1973). (ERIC Document Reproduction Service No. ED 145 488)

J. C. Penney Company, Inc. (1984). *Consumer Feedback '84.* New York: Author.

J. C. Penney Company, Inc. (1985). *Consumer Feedback '85.* New York: Author.

Jecklin, Mary Jean, & Fetter, Elizabeth A. (1985). *Needs of older employees and retirees: Task force results of the Corporate Volunteerism Council of Minneapolis and St. Paul, Minnesota.* Minneapolis/St. Paul, MN: Corporate Volunteerism Council. (ERIC Document Reproduction Service No. ED 265 285)

Joint Committee on Standards for Educational Evaluation. (1981). *Standards for evaluaions of educational programs, projects, and materials.* New York: McGraw-Hill.

Jourard, Sidney M. (1964). *The transparent self.* Princeton, NJ: D. Van Nostrand.

Kahan, Hazel, Davies, John O., III, & Wilson, Jay F. (1982, May 14). Professional respondents say they're better for research than virgins, but they're not and focus groups need new focus, changes in their facilities, moderator strategy, marketing. *Marketing News,* pp. 22-23.

Kahaner, Larry. (1986, March 17). When MCI tested the ad waters. *Advertising Age,* p. 56.

Kalasunas, Michael P. (1985-1986). Agency research: Myth and legend. *Journal of Advertising Research, 25*(6), RC6-RC10.

Karger, Ted. (1987, August 28). Focus groups are for focusing, and for little else. *Marketing News,* pp. 52-55.

Katz, Daniel, Gutek, Barbara A., Kahn, Robert L., & Barton, Eugenia. (1975). *Bureaucratic encounters.* Ann Arbor: University of Michigan, Institute for Social Research.

Katz, Martin. (1984, January 6). Selecting the right research firm: Step-by-step guidelines. *Marketing News,* pp. 1, 27.

Kelleher, Joanne. (1982). Find out what your customers really want. *Inc, 4*(1), 88, 91.

Keller, Keryl Lynn. (1986). Beliefs about and needs of persons 65 years of age and over: Focus group interviews with senior citizens and baby boom groups. (Doctoral dissertation, Southern Illinois University, Carbondale, 1986). *Dissertation Abstracts International, 47,* (7-A) 2468.

Keown, Charles. (1983). Focus group research: Tool for the retailer. *Journal of Small Business Management, 21*(2), 59-65.

Key role of research in Agree's success is told. (1979, January 12). *Marketing News*, pp. 14-15.

Kirk, Jerome, & Miller, Marc L. (1986). *Reliability and validity in qualitative research.* Beverly Hills, CA: Sage.

Kleimenhagen, Arno, & Cavusgil, S. Tamer. (1982, June 25). Financial counselors should adopt sequential screening approach when recruiting clients. *Marketing News*, pp. 3-4.

Klein, Frederick C. (1983, July 7). Research probes consumer using anthropological skills. *The Wall Street Journal*, p. 21.

Kopee, Joseph A. (1982). The communication audit. *Public Relations Journal, 38*(5), 24-27.

Kover, Arthur J. (1982-1983). Point of view: The legitimacy of qualitative research. *Journal of Advertising Research, 22*(6), 49-50.

Kraft, Larine. (1981). Focus groups: Letting consumers think about your new product idea. *Food Technology, 35*(11), 70-72.

Krueger, Richard A. (1984). *Focus group interviewing as an evaluation tool.* Paper presented at the Evaluation Research Society & Evaluation Network Annual Meeting, San Francisco.

Krueger, Richard A. (1986). Focus group interviewing: A helpful technique for agricultural educators. *The Visitor, 73*(1). (St. Paul: University of Minnesota, Division of Agricultural Education)

Krueger, Richard A., & Hutchins, Ardis Cook. (1986). Group interviews focus on good design. *Architecture Minnesota, 12*(5), 25.

Krueger, Richard A., Hutchins, Ardis Cook, & Olney, Gail D. (1985). *Focus group interviewing for architects and interior designers.* St. Paul: Research in Design.

Krueger, Richard A., Mueller, Marsha R., & Casey, Mary Anne. (1986). *An assessment of farm credit mediation.* St. Paul: University of Minnesota, Minnesota Extension Service.

Kunimoto, Sandra L. (1986). *Consumer perceptions of Kona Coffee.* Unpublished manuscript, University of Hawaii, Honolulu.

Labaw, Patricia. (1985) *Advanced questionnaire design.* Cambridge, MA: Ballinger.

Lacey, Diane. (1984, April). Management technology: The future . . . without the shock. *Marketing & Media Decisions*, pp. 74-79.

Lambert, David. (1986, February 28). Consumers, physicians air views on IPAs. *Marketing News*, pp. 20-21.

Langer, Judith. (1978, September 8). Clients: Check qualitative researcher's personal traits to get more: Qualitative researchers: Enter entire marketing process to give more. *Marketing News*, pp. 10-11.

Langer, Judith. (1979, September 21). 12 Keys to unlock qualitative research on sensitive subjects. *Marketing News*, pp. 10, 20.

Langer, Judith. (1984). Piercing the smoke screen. *Nation's Business, 72*(8), 24.

Langer, Judith. (1985, September 13). Story time is alternative research technique. *Marketing News*, pp. 19, 24.

Langer, Judith, & Miller, Susan. (1985). The ideal focus group facility. *Journal of Data Collection, 25*(2), 34-37.

LaPiere, R. T. (1934). Attitudes and actions. *Social Forces, 13*, 230-237.

Lareau, Marybeth. (1983). Consumer: Women torn between two stereotypes. *Madison Avenue, 25*(8), 28-33.

LaTour, Stephen A., Friedman, Bernard, & Hughes, Edward F. X. (1986). Medical beneficiary decision making about health insurance. *Medical Care, 24*(7), 601-614.

Lavidge, Robert J. (1984). Nine tested ways to mislead product planners. *Journal of Product Innovation Management, 2,* 101-105.

Lazarfeld, Paul. (1986). The art of asking why. New York: The Advertising Research Foundation. (Original work published 1934, in *The National Marketing Review*)

Lederman, Linda C. (1982). Suffering in silence: The effects of fear of talking on small group participation. *Group & Organization Studies, 7*(3), 279-294.

Lederman, Linda C. (1983). High communication apprehensives talk about communication apprehension and its effects on their behavior. *Communication Quarterly, 31*(3), 233-237.

Lee, Jeanne. (1981). *Using new methods to determine continuing education needs of rural women.* (ERIC Document Reproduction Service No. ED 233 131)

Leonhard, Dietz. (1975, October 10). Can focus group interviews survive? *Marketing News,* pp. 6-7.

Leven, Nora. (1983). *Computer education needs for an agricultural application.* St. Paul: University of Minnesota, Office of Special Programs.

Levy, Mark R. (1982). The Lazarsfeld-Stanton Program Analyzer: An historical note. *Journal of Communication, 32*(4), 30-38.

*Levy, Sidney J. (1979). Focus group interviewing. In James B. Higginbotham & Keith K. Cox (Eds.), *Focus group interviews: A reader.* Chicago: American Marketing Association.

Lincoln, Rhonda M. (1987). *Special interest programs for Expanded Food and Nutrition Education graduates.* Unpublished manuscript, Kahului, University of Hawaii, Maui County Extension Service.

Lincoln, Yvonna S., & Guba, Egon G. (1985). *Naturalistic inquiry.* Beverly Hills, CA: Sage.

Linda, Gerald. (1982). Focus groups: A new look at an old friend. *Marketing & Media Decisions, 17*(10), 96, 98.

Lindgren, John H., Jr., & Kehoe, William J. (1981). Focus groups: Approaches, procedures, and implications. *Journal of Retail Banking, 3*(4), 16-22.

Lipstein, Benjamin, & Neelankavil, James P. (1984). Television advertising copy research: A critical review of the state of the art. *Journal of Advertising Research, 24*(2), 19-25.

Little, Michael W., & Easley, Eddie V. (1982, January 22). Banks can conduct focus groups to analyze market opportunities. *Marketing News,* pp. 20, 22.

Lometti, Guy, & Feig, Ellen. (1984). The day after. Caring about children: The role of audience research. *Television & Children, 7*(1), 32-36.

Long, James S. (1983, October). *An evaluation of the focused group interview as an adult education needs assessment technique.* Paper presented at the annual meeting of the Evaluation Research Society and the Evaluation Network, Chicago.

Long, James S., & Marts, Julia Ann. (1981). *The focused group interview: An alternative way to collect information to evaluation conferences.* Unpublished manuscript, Pullman, Washington State Cooperative Extension Service.

Lorz, F. Michael. (1984). Focus group research in a winning campaign. *Public Relations Review, 10*(2), 28-38.

Lubet, Margery J. (1982). Focus group research: Planning is the key. *Bank Marketing, 14*(12), 17-20.

Lydecker, Toni H. (1986). Focus group dynamics. *Association Management, 38*(3), 73-78.

Maher, Thomas M. (1986). Met life focusing on Asian Americans. *National Underwriter (Life/Health), 90*(14), 4, 8.

Mann, Ned. (1986). To create and keep a customer. *Managers Magazine, 61*(3), 10-13.

Mariampolski, Hy. (1984). The resurgence of qualitative research. *Public Relations Journal, 40*(7), 21-23.

Market testing by group interview. (1962, December 7). *Printer's Ink*, pp. 66-67.

Markey, Karen. (1983, March). *Online catalog use: Results of surveys and focus group interviews in several libraries: Vol. 2. Final Report* (Report No. OCLC/OPR/RR-83/3). Dublin, OH: Online Computer Library Center, Inc. (ERIC Document Reproduction Service No. ED 231 403)

Matheson, Richard E. (1983, May 13). Qualitative research methods (other than focus groups) can provide valuable information. *Marketing News*, p. 14.

*McDaniel, Carl. (1979). Focus groups: Their role in the marketing research process. *Akron Business & Economic Review, 10*(4), 14-19.

McDermott, Dennis R. (1985). A market research analysis of an adolescent in-patient substance abuse program. *Health Marketing Quarterly, 2*(4), 51-57.

McDermott, Dennis R. (1987). Assessing future directions for designing an academic program through focus group interviews. *Journal of Professional Services Marketing, 2*(4), 113-118.

McDonald, William J. (1982). Approaches to group research with children. *Journal of the Academy of Marketing Science, 10*(4), 490-499.

McQuarrie, Edward F., & McIntyre, Shelby H. (1986). Focus groups and the development of new products by technologically driven companies: Some guidelines. *Journal of Product Innovation Management, 3*(1), 40-47.

McQuarrie, Edward F, & McIntyre, Shelby H. (1987). What focus groups can and cannot do: A reply to Seymour. *Journal of Product Innovation Management, 4*(1), 55-60.

Merton, Robert K. (1987). The focused interview and focus groups: Continuities and discontinuities. *Public Opinion Quarterly. 51*(4), 550-556.

*Merton, Robert K., Fiske, Marjorie, & Kendall, Patricia L. (1956). *The focused interview.* Glencoe, IL: Free Press.

Meyers, Barbara E. (1984). New product development: Can technique substitute for technology? *Bulletin of the American Society for Information Science, 10*(5), 13-15.

Minnesota Extension Service. (1985). *Focus group interview report: Nicollet County Extension Service.* Unpublished manuscript, St. Paul, University of Minnesota, Extension Service.

Miskovic, Darlene. (1980, November 17). Behind the mirror. *Advertising Age*, p. 55.

Moorefield, James L. (1985). Health insurers look to mid-1990s. *National Underwriter (Life/Health), 89*(22), 3, 38.

Moran, William T. (1986). The science of qualitative research. *Journal of Advertising Research, 26*(3), RC16-RC19.

Morgan, David L., & Spanish, Margaret T. (1984). Focus groups: A new tool for qualitative research. *Qualitative Sociology, 7*(3), 253-270.

Morris, Lynn Lyons, & Fitz-Gibbon, Carol Taylor. (1978). *How to present an evaluation report.* Beverly Hills, CA: Sage.

Morris, Lynn Lyons, Fitz-Gibbon, Carol Taylor, Freeman, Marie E. (1987). *How to communicate evaluation findings.* Newbury Park, CA: Sage.

Moss, Lynn M. (1982, November 26). Consensor's "visual feedback" of opinions could revolutionize focus group research. *Marketing News*, p. 6.

Mueller, Marsha R. (1987). *Qualitative evaluation: Analysis issues for the occasional evaluator.* Unpublished manuscript.

Mueller, Marsha R., & Anderson, Eugene. (1985). *Report of three focus group interviews held with commercial farm families in northwestern Minnesota.* St. Paul: University of Minnesota, Agricultural Extension Service, Office of Special Programs.

Mueller, Marsha R., & Krueger, Richard A. (1985, October). *Qualitative evaluation from a utilization focused perspective: The Minnesota experience.* Paper presented at the Joint Meeting of Evaluation Research Society and Evaluation Network, Toronto, Canada. (ERIC Document Reproduction Service No. ED 267 104)

Mullis, R. M., & Lansing, D. (1986). Using focus groups to plan worksite nutrition programs. *Journal of Nutrition Education, 18*(2), S32-S34.

Munn, Henry L., & Opdyke, William L. (1961, Fall). Group interviews reveal consumer buying behavior. *Journal of Retailing,* pp. 26-31.

Murphy, Patrick E., & Laczniak, Gene R. (1982, July 23). How marketing educators, text authors can give higher priority to ethics issues. *Marketing News,* p. 14.

Murphy, Paul. (1983). Research methods increase bottom line payoff. *Direct Marketing, 45*(11), 40-60.

Naffziger, Douglas W. (1986). The smooth transition. *Training & Development Journal, 40*(4), 63-65.

Nakamura, Charlotte W. (1987). *Innovative programmatic thrusts to teach non-traditional audiences in extension home economics.* Unpublished paper, Maui County Extension Service, Kahului, Hawaii.

National Institute of Health. (1978). *Report to the national high blood pressure education program.* Prepared under contract by Porter, Novelli, & Associates, Bethesda, MD.

Nebraska University, Lincoln. (1979). *A summary of research on potential educational markets for videodisc programming.* (ERIC Document Reproduction Service No. ED 234 760)

Neuman, Susan B. (1985, May). *The uses of reading mass-produced fiction.* Paper presented at the annual meeting of the International Reading Association, New Orleans, LA. (ERIC Document Reproduction Service No. ED 263 528)

Newbold, Patricia L. (1981, June). *Research study to assess individual and vocational program needs for adult education. Final Report.* Pittsburgh, PA: Associated Educational Consultants, Inc. (ERIC Document Reproduction Service No. ED 206 930)

Newman, Jan H. (1979, September 21). Husband-wife focus groups help let the voice of the family be heard. *Marketing News,* p. 2.

News media credibility a problem for marketers. (1986, January 3). *Marketing News,* p. 58.

Now we're group focusing. (1986, September-October). *Minnesota,* p. 5. (Minneapolis: University of Minnesota Alumni Association)

Olmstead, Marty. (1985). Nestle mails the very best. *Sales & Marketing Mgmt, 134*(1), 49-50.

Overholser, Charles. (1986). Quality, quantity, and thinking real hard. *Journal of Advertising Research, 26*(3), RC7-RC12.

Parasuraman, A., Zeithaml, Valarie A., & Berry, Leonard L. (1985). A conceptual model of service quality and its implications for future research. *Journal of Marketing, 49*(4), 41-50.

Paskowski, Marianne. (1981). Psycho-marketing: Industrial advertisers lag behind state-of-the-art. *Industrial Marketing, 66*(7), 40-48.

Patton, Michael Q. (1980). *Qualitative evaluation methods.* Beverly Hills, CA: Sage.

Patton, Michael Q. (1982). *Practical evaluation.* Beverly Hills, CA: Sage.

Patton, Michael Q. (1986). *Utilization focused evaluation.* Beverly Hills, CA: Sage.

Peterson, Roland L., & Migler, Jerry R. (1987) *Adjusting post-secondary agriculture curriculum to promote educational access: An experiment.* St. Paul: University of Minnesota, Department of Vocational and Technical Education.

Phone conferencing touted as cost-effective alternative to in-person focus group research. (1980, May 16). *Marketing News,* pp. 11, 13.

Pomerance, Eugene C. (1982, September 17). Don't use misleading term "qualitative research"; "Exploratory" and "explanatory" are more precise. *Marketing News,* pp. 16, 18.

Pope, Jeff. (1977, July 11). Six ways to improve today's focus group research. *Advertising Age,* pp. 150, 152.

Pramualratana, Anthony, Havanon, Napaporn, & Knodel, John. (1985). Exploring the normative basis for age at marriage in Thailand: An example from focus group research. *Journal of Marriage and the Family, 47*(1), 203-210.

Prince, Melvin. (1979, September 8). Focus groups can give marketer early clues on marketability of new product. *Marketing News,* p. 12.

Profs get primer in use, problems of focus groups. (1986, September 12). *Marketing News,* p. 36.

Quaker State expects sales gains with new packaging system for oil. (1984, February 3). *Marketing News,* p. 7.

Qualitative is marketing research because it aids decision makers, helps reduce risk. (1982, January 22). *Marketing News,* p. 8.

Quann, Byron G. (1985). How IBM assesses its business-to-business advertising. *Business Marketing, 70*(1), 106-112.

Quiriconi, Roy. (1975, July 18). Focusing on focus group moderators: Some thoughts on how to avoid "tape recorder carriers" who "do focus groups." *Marketing News,* p. 6.

Quiriconi, Roy J. (1978, January 27). Calder's three approaches offer a way to get a sharper focus on focus groups. *Marketing News,* p. 12.

Quiriconi, Roy J., & Dorgan, Richard E. (1985). Respondent personalities: Insight for better focus groups. *Journal of Data Collection, 25*(2), 20-23.

Reach for the stars. (1986, February 17). *Newsweek,* p. 8.

Reece, Richard L. (1985a, January). Corporate transformation of medicine in Minnesota: How physicians think, or lessons learned from focus group discussions with 150 physicians. *Minnesota Medicine,* pp. 9-12.

Reece, Richard L. (1985b, February). The corporate transformation of medicine in Minnesota: How hospital administrators think. Focus group findings. *Minnesota Medicine,* pp. 87-93.

Reed, John G. (1984). Effective customer relation. *Telephone Engineer & Management, 88*(10), 102-105.

Reitman, Judith. (1985). Keeping an eye on media habits. *Marketing & Media Decisions, 20*(9), 128-132.

Research buyers of major corporations tell why, how they use focus groups, work to avoid or solve problems groups might cause. (1976, January 16). *Marketing News,* pp. 1, 12-14, 17, 21.

Research methodology detailed for repositioning mature brands. (1983, June 24). *Marketing News,* p. 11.

Reynolds, Fred D., & Johnson, Deborah K. (1978). Validity of focus group findings. *Journal of Advertising Research, 18*(3), 21-24.

Rhodes, Wayne L., Jr. (1983). The information center extends a helping hand. *Infosystems, 30*(1), 26-27, 30.

Rice, James A., & Taylor, Susan. (1984, February). Assessing the market for long-term care services. *Healthcare Financial Management, 38*(2), 32-46.

Rice, S. A. (Ed.). (1931). *Methods in social science.* Chicago: University of Chicago Press.

Rigler, Edith. (1987). Focus on focus groups. *ABA Banking Journal, 97*(4), 96-100.

Roethlisberger, F. J., & Dickson, W. J. (1938). *Management and the worker.* Cambridge, MA: Harvard University Press.

Rogers, Carl R. (1942). *Counseling and psychotherapy.* New York: Houghton Mifflin.

Roller, Margaret R. (1984, September 14). Use this checklist to select research firm. *Marketing News*, p. 25.

Roller, Margaret R. (1985, November 8). Mental image of groups is out of focus. *Marketing News*, pp. 21, 26.

Roseman, Edward. (1986). Designing promotion for the prospect under pressure. *Medical Marketing & Media, 21*(3), 58-63.

Rosendahl, Iris. (1986). What young mothers think about drugstores. *Drug Topics, 130*(5), 68-75.

Rosenstein, Alvin J. (1976, May 21). Quantitative—Yes, quantitative—applications for the focus group. *Marketing News*, p. 8.

Rossell, Christine A. (1986). Research pays off. *ZIP/Target Marketing, 9*(5), 26, 28.

Rostky, George. (1986). Unveiling market segments with technical focus research. *Business Marketing, 7*(10), 66, 68.

Russo, N. (1967). Connotation of seating arrangement. *Cornell Journal of Social Relations, 2*, 37-44.

Schleier, Curt. (1985, November 14). Lawyers court help in jury selection, legal cases. *Advertising Age*, pp. 30-32.

Schnee, Robert K. (1982, January 22). Follow these 6 rules when doing qualitative research for evaluating new product ideas. *Marketing News*, p. 22.

Schwartz, Martin L., Jolson, Marvin A., & Lee, Ronald H. (1986). The marketing of funeral services: Past, present, and future. *Business Horizons, 29*(2), 40-45.

Scotti, Dennis J., Bonner, P. Greg, & Wiman, Alan R. (1986). An analysis of the determinants of HMO re-enrollment behavior: Implications for theory and policy. *Journal of Health Care Marketing, 6*(2), 7-16.

Scotti, Dennis J., Gluck, G. M., Maykow, K. P., Lakin, L. B., & Triano, C. (1986). Psychosocial factors in utilization of dental services among the noninstitutional elderly: An exploratory focus group-analysis. *Journal of Public Health Dentistry, 46*(1), 73.

Serafin, Raymond. (1986, March 13). Awaiting Allante: Cadillac rides with Pininfarina in ultraluxury. *Advertising Age*, pp. 4-5.

Service-charge debate. (1985). *Credit Union Magazine, 51*(5), 46-50.

Seymour, Daniel T. (1983). The trade-offs of focus group research. *Bank Marketing, 15*(4), 19-20, 22.

Seymour, Daniel T. (1987). Focus groups and the development of new products by technologically driven companies: A comment. *Journal of Product Innovation Management, 4*(1), 50-54.

Shaw, Marvin E. (1976). *Group dynamics: The psychology of small group behavior.* New York: McGraw-Hill.

Sherry, John F. (1983). Gift giving in anthropological perspective. *Journal of Consumer Research, 10*(2), 157-168.

Shoddy, recruiting practices lead to focus group biases. (1979, May 18). *Marketing News*, p. 3.

Shrawder, J. Edward. (1985, September 13). Some consumer research valid in business markets. *Marketing News*, pp. 41, 43, 49.

Simon, Murray. (1987, January 30). Physician focus groups require special techniques. *Marketing News*, pp. 21-22.

Small CUs: Their future's at stake. (1985). *Credit Union Magazine, 51*(7), 66-70.

Smith, Alexa. (1984). Have you QMRed your media lately? *Marketing & Media Decisions, 19*(2), 90, 92.

Smith, Alexa. (1986, September 12). Researchers must control focus group—and those behind the mirror as well. *Marketing News*, pp. 33-34, 36.

Sokolow, Hal. (1985, September 13). In-depth interviews increasing in importance. *Marketing News*, pp. 26, 31.

Stephenson, W. E. (1984). A poll is not a prop. *Communication World, 9*, 36-37.

Stevens, Mark. (1986, July 11). Focus groups help companies read their customers' minds. *Minneapolis Star and Tribune*, p. 12B.

Strother, Raymond D. (1984, July 2). Voters' bias shuts door on female leaders. *Minneapolis Star and Tribune*, p. 9A.

Studies in Family Planning. (1981). Focus group research [Special issue]. *12*(12), 407-456.

Stycos, J. M. (1981). A critique of focus group and survey research: The machismo case. *Studies in Family Planning, 12*(12), 450-456.

Sullivan, Nick. (1983). Blue-collar workers climb back into the limelight. *Ad Forum, 4*(3), 10-11, 53-54.

Surveys' objective: To improve focus group studies: Calder. (1978, October 20). *Marketing News*, pp. 1, 5.

Szybillo, George J., & Berger, Robert. (1979). What advertising agencies think of focus groups. *Journal of Advertising Research, 19*(3), 29-33.

Taylor, Steven J., & Robert Bogdan. (1984). *Introduction to qualitative research methods: The search for meanings* (2nd ed.). New York: John Wiley.

Teweles, Gillian. (1985). Brand management: Carter cottons to women. *Madison Avenue, 27*(6), 20, 22.

Thompson, Terrence N. (1979, March 12). Focus groups are marketing research and other fallacies. *Marketing News.*

Thompson, Thomas W., & Rush, Patrick A. (1985/1986, Winter). Improving bank/media relations. *Journal of Retail Banking, 7*(4), 33-42.

Timex and VALS engineer a psychographic product launch. (1984). *Ad Forum, 5*(9), 12-14.

Tootikian, Lawrence. (1983). Readership research. *Publishing Trade, 2*(5), 24-28.

Trachtenberg, Jeffery A. (1987, October 5). Listening, the old-fashioned way. *Forbes*, pp. 202, 204.

Urbanski, Al. (1985). Potato clocks and fancy boxes. *Sales & Marketing Management, 134*(5), 73-76.

Vanderveer, Richard B. (1987). Beyond focus groups: A thrift's guide to market research. *Bottomline, 4*(7), 33-38.

Van de Vall, Mark, Bolas, Cheryl, & Kang, Tai S. (1976). Applied social research in industrial organizations: An evaluation of functions, theory, and methods. *Journal of Applied Behavioral Science, 12*, 158-177.

Vavra, Terry G., & Thorbeck, John. (1983, September 16). Cut recruiting costs, gather vivid information with "on-site" qualitative research technique. *Marketing News*, pp. 18, 19.

Vichas, Robert P. (1983). 11 ways focus groups produce profit-making ideas. *Marketing Times, 30*(2), 17-18.

Walker, Robert (Ed.). (1985). *Applied qualitative research*. Brookfield, VT: Gower.

Walters, Pamela Barnhouse. (1977, April). *Development and production leading to a television series on parent education. An assessment of parent education and general needs that can be served by educational programming for television. Final report.* Silver Spring, MD: Applied Management Sciences, Inc. (ERIC Document Reproduction Service No. ED 206 268)

Watson, Claire. (1983). Participation in a focus group. *National Intravenous Therapy Association, 6*, 402-403.

Weisberger, Fran. (1985). Technological advancements in newspapers. *Marketing & Media Decisions, 20*(10), pp. 80, 82.

Weiss, Carol H. (1976). Policy research in the university: Practical aid or academic exercise? *Policy Studies Journal, 4*(3), 224-233.

*Welch, Joe L. (1985a). Focus groups for restaurant research. *Cornell Hotel and Restaurant Association Quarterly, 26*(2), 78-85.

*Welch, Joe L. (1985b). Researching marketing problems and opportunities with focus groups. *Industrial Marketing Management, 14*(4), 245-253.

*Wells, William D. (1974). Group interviewing. In Robert Ferber (Ed.), *Handbook of marketing research*. New York: McGraw-Hill. (Reprinted in James B. Higginbotham, & Keith K. Cox, 1979. *Focus group interviews: A reader*. Chicago: American Marketing Association)

When using qualitative research to generate new product ideas, ask these five questions. (1982, May 14). *Marketing News*, p. 15.

Whittington, Marna C., & Benson, Stephen D. (1975). *Identification of barriers and proposed solutions to the attainment of equal representation in post-secondary allied health programs for minorities. Final Report.* Philadelphia, PA: Associates for Research in Behavior, Inc. (ERIC Document Reproduction Service No. ED 118 299)

Wilson, Aubrey. (1984, June). Innovation in the marketplace. *Management Today (UK)*, pp. 78-82.

Wolff, Mark R. (1988). Focus groups for the market-driven. *Bottomline, 5*(1), 55-56.

Women aren't the only ones changing: Marketers should take note of men, too. (1983, July 22). *Marketing News*, p. 13.

Yankelovitch, Skelly and White, Inc. (1977). *The General Mills American family report 1976-77: Raising children in a changing society*. New York. (ERIC Document Reproduction Service No. ED 145 298)

Yin, Robert K. (1984). *Case study research*. Beverly Hills, CA: Sage.

Yoshino, Rhoda M. (1987). *Feasibility study of a new educational program: Promotion of island grown vegetables*. Unpublished manuscript, Honolulu, University of Hawaii, Ohau County Extension Service.

Zanes, Ruth L. (1979, September 21). Recruiting friends, other shortcuts are stealing; Don't pay for such responses. *Marketing News*, p. 4.

Zemke, Ron. (1978). How market research techniques can pay off for trainers. *Training, 15*(12), 48-49.

Zimmerman, Juliet G., & Zeinio, Robert N. (1985). Listening is the key to more productive focus group sessions. *Medical Marketing & Media, 20*(10), 84-88.

Index

About the Author

Richard A. Krueger is Professor and Extension Evaluation Specialist at the University of Minnesota. He holds the baccalaureate degree in history from Bethel College (1964), the master's degree in public affairs from the University of Minnesota (1971), and the doctorate in education from the University of Minnesota (1979). He has worked on a variety of evaluation projects relating to nutrition, rural economic recovery, chemical dependency, community development, and volunteer participation, to name a few. He regularly teaches evaluation classes at the University of Minnesota, where he serves as Adjunct Professor in the Department of Vocational and Technical Education. In his role as Extension Evaluation Specialist, he provides statewide leadership in program evaluation for the Minnesota Extension Service. In 1987, he served as Visiting Professor at the University of Hawaii.

NOTES

NOTES

NOTES